THE COMPLEAT IMBIBER ELEVEN

The Complea

Imbiber Eleven

Fabiano

Souper de Gourmet

Une petite caille, des fruits, du champagne : Monsieur est servi !

(*Dessin de* R. PRÉJELAN.)

From an old copy of LA VIE PARISIENNE c 1905

Entertainment

Edited by CYRIL RAY

Designed by CHARLES HASLER

HUTCHINSON OF LONDON

RIGHT: A vineyard near Meursault

F. S. Matta Limited,
who sponsor the eleventh issue of *The Compleat Imbiber*,
offer this compendium of entertainment and information
to all amateurs of wine and good living.
The Compleat Imbiber, which was first published in book form in
1956, has been edited since by Cyril Ray.

Published 1970 by
Hutchinson and Company (Publishers) Limited
178–202 Great Portland Street, London W1
London Melbourne Sydney Auckland Johannesburg Cape Town
and agencies throughout the world

The text of this book is set in 11 pt Monotype Scotch Roman
Made and printed in Great Britain by
Anchor Press, and bound by William Brendon,
both of Tiptree, Essex

ISBN 0 09 104490 1

On the two preceding pages

André Bouchant, 1873–1958
LA MISE EN BOUTEILLES
Oil on canvas (60cm × 73cm) painted 1948

In the collection of David G. Smith Esq.

André Bouchant was born at Châteaurenault (Indre-et-Loire) not very far from Tours, on 24 April 1873. His father, Julien, was a gardener, vine grower, and nurseryman, and André became an apprentice in these same skills in 1890.

His service in World War I led him toward cartography, drawing, and painting, and on demobilisation in 1919 he decided to become a painter. In 1921 he sent sixteen works to the Salon d'Automne, had nine accepted, and became acquainted with Le Corbusier, who was the first to buy his work. Shortly after he was commissioned to design the decor and costumes for the ballet *Apollon Musagète*.

His work covered a wide range of subject matter, and included portraits and figure compositions, and he often returned to his former 'professional' subjects of flowers and trees, these last always forming an important element in his figure compositions.

Several exhibitions of his work have been held in Europe, and as far afield as Tokyo and New York, several of them since his death on 12 August 1958. The most recent exhibition was held at the Mayor Gallery, London, in the autumn of 1969, in which *La Mise en Bouteilles* was included and which is here reproduced by kind permission of the present owner.

Contents

Acknowledgements

As usual, many people have helped in the preparation of this volume, and grateful acknowledgement is made to those mentioned below.

The editors of: *The Guardian* for Charles Parr's *Snakes Chop Suey*: *Punch* for Alan Brien's *Strictly from Hunger,* and E. S. Turner's *Petit Tour de France: The Listener* for Adrian Mitchell's *Gastronomic Pornography*: the *Sunday Times* for Hugh Johnson's *Confessions of a Merman*: and the *Spectator* for Vernon Watkins's *For a Wise Festival.*

Especial thanks are also due to David G. Smith for André Bouchant's painting *La Mise en Bouteilles*: the Ferrers Gallery, London, for the Helleu drypoint in Anthony Powell's article on Proust and the Cheret posters in *Marcel's Paris*: and Alec Davis for many of the illustrations to Elizabeth Ray's article on sauces.

For other pictorial material – the Franklin Printing Company, Philadelphia: Radio Times Hulton Picture Library: Le Jardin des Gourmets: Boulestin's Restaurant: The Savoy Hotel: New College, Oxford: Jesus College, Cambridge: the French Tourist Office: Interfoto MTI Budapest: Bremer Ratskeller: Guy Gravett: *Le Guide Michelin*: *Punch*: and many others, unknown, whose work has been included.

CYRIL RAY

Introduction

NY ANTHOLOGY
of good living must inevitably
range fairly widely in its search for good writing about fine wines
and rare dishes. But more even than usual, I think, this eleventh
issue of our more or less annual entertainment has taken on an
international air.

Henri Gault and Christian Millau, certainly, the authors of those
two remarkable Julliard gastronomic guides – one to Paris, and
one, the even more remarkable of the two, to London – have
combed the world before deciding, predictably, that its best
restaurants are in France. It is nice to think that I knew the
Troisgros at Roanne, which they praise so highly, before it had a
single Michelin star: now it has three. Indeed when the late Ernest
Atkinson and I dined there with our respective wives a dozen or
more years ago, and congratulated one of the brothers on the
superb food and service, he brought the other brother and his
father to share our compliments, and asked us shyly if we could
bring ourselves to write to Michelin and say as much to the editor
of the Guide. We both did so – they deserved it – and may well
have helped their first steps on the road to fame.

As well as the great range of restaurants that the Julliard
gastronomes discuss here, there is a German wine-cellar and an old
champagne house; prunes are celebrated this year, as well as

LEFT: *The Old Bell* at Hurley, mentioned by Robin McDouall

paprika; Alan Brien's American browsings seem in their way no less exotic than Charles Parr's snakes chop suey; and Robin McDouall's first gastronomic excursions seem now almost as far away in time as those others are in space.

That most American of drinks, the mint julep, is annually celebrated, we learn, at New College, but I have discovered since Dermot Morrah sent me his learned article that its fame had reached these shores before the first New College Mint Julep Night in 1845.

After the success of *Mr Midshipman Easy* and his other novels, Captain Frederick Marryat, R.N., spent the years 1837 to 1839 in Canada and the United States, with the intention of writing a book comparing the British and the American systems of government. This six-volume *Diary in America, with Remarks on its Institutions* appeared in 1839, and the account in it of how to make a mint julep disposes of the belief, which I once shared with New College, that the traditional, as distinct from the currently accepted, recipe calls for Kentucky bourbon. (Nowadays experts are as likely as I see from Mr Morrah's article that M. André Simon is to specify rye whiskey: bourbon is, of course, made from corn.) It is also written in a tone notably magnanimous in one who had just been burned in effigy in Detroit, 'variously accused', says the reference book of Captain Marryat, 'of assaulting women, insulting Henry Clay, and being a spy'.

'. . . I must descant a little upon the mint julep', the captain wrote, 'as it is, with the thermometer at 100 degrees, one of the most delightful and insinuating potations that ever was invented, and may be drunk with equal satisfaction when the thermometer is as low as 70 degrees. There are many varieties, such as those composed of claret, Madeira, etc; but the ingredients of the real mint julep are as follows. I learned how to make them, and succeeded pretty well. Put into a tumbler about a dozen sprigs of the tender shoots of mint, upon them put a spoonful of white sugar, and equal proportions of peach and common brandy* so as to fill it up one-third or perhaps a little less. Then take rasped or pounded ice, and fill up the tumbler. Epicures rub the lip of the tumbler with a piece of fresh pineapple, and the tumbler itself is very often incrusted outside with stalactites of ice. As the ice melts, you drink.

* *Try all brandy.* C.R.

16

'I once heard two ladies talking in the next room to me, and
one of them said, "Well, if I have a weakness for any one thing,
it is for a mint julep!" – a very amiable weakness, and proving
her good sense and good taste. They are, in fact, like all
American ladies, irresistible! . . .'

Perhaps there was something in one, at any rate, of those Detroit
accusations against the gallant captain.

Eliza Acton, too, in her *Modern Cookery for Private Families*,
published in 1845 and dedicated to 'The Young Housekeepers of
England', recommended 'wine, brandy, or any other spirit' in her
receipt for mint julep, which she poured 'from one tumbler to the
other until the whole is sufficiently impregnated with the flavour
of the mint, which is extracted by the particles of the ice coming
into brisk contact when changed from one vessel to the other'.
Adding, though, that 'we apprehend that this preparation is, like
most other iced beverages, to be imbibed through a reed; the
receipt, which was contributed by an American gentleman, is
somewhat vague.'

No doubt.

But although Captain Marryat in the eighteen-thirties and Miss
Acton in the eighteen-forties were making their juleps with brandy,
it was whisky that went into the mint juleps with which a
Washington doctor ministered to William Howard Russell of *The
Times*, recovering from the heat, the smells and the fatigue after
witnessing and reporting the panic-stricken rout of the Northern
armies at First Bull Run in 1861.

The doctor prescribed 'powders in mint juleps', and although
Russell did not record *what* powders, he wrote:

'. . . Now mint juleps are made of whisky, sugar, ice, very little
water, and sprigs of fresh mint, to be sucked up after the
manner of sherry cobblers, if so it be pleased, with a straw. "A
powder every two hours, with a mint julep. Why, that's six a
day, doctor! Won't that be – eh? – won't that be rather
intoxicating?" "Well, sir, that depends on the constitution. You'll
find they will do you no harm, even if the worst takes place." . . .'

No harm, even if the worst takes place: the editor confidently
commends this year's IMBIBER, in the same comforting spirit.

ROBIN MCDOUALL

The Gay
Gastronomic

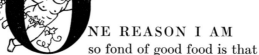

NE REASON I AM
so fond of good food is that
at three periods of my life I was subjected to really bad cooking.
The first was in my grandmother's house during the 1914–18
war. No doubt this was partly due to rationing – I can remember
each person's different coloured saucer with his or her ration of
butter for the week – but I think it was due more to my grandmother's positive dislike of good food. She had been born and lived
most of her adult life in India, married to my Bengal Lancer
grandfather. Years of hot curries had paralysed her taste-buds.
Her favourite breakfast dish was *dhal blatt* (boiled lentils and rice);
her favourite joint, boiled mutton and caper sauce; her favourite
pudding, 'shape'. The same 'white sauce' – what my sister and I
called 'photo-paste' – covered cauliflower, beetroot, fish, eggs,
chicken, veal, and puddings. Once a year, on my birthday, Mrs
Scotchings, the cook, who ordinarily carried out her wishes to a T,
made me a chestnut pudding (Monte Bianco), surrounded by
whipped cream and covered with spun sugar. Was Mrs Scotchings
really a wonderful cook, hiding her light under my grandmother's
bushel?

The next stage of really staggeringly bad food was at Haileybury.
Breakfast and tea were tolerable, as we were allowed our own jam,
marmalade, honey, butter and potted meat, for which I had an
account at the local grocer. I do not remember ever eating the
school luncheon. I also had an account with the tuck-shop and

18

wenties

used to buy a hot roll, two packets of Smith's Crisps and a bar of Sharp's Super-Kreem Toffee. On Saturdays we were allowed to eat in our studies, and used then to have a huge fry-up of eggs, bacon and sausages.

My third period of uneatable food was in the winter of 1939–40. My R.A.F. unit was housed in a hutted army camp outside Carlisle. Sweet-rationing in the services was not too bad and one kept going on Kit-Kat bars and cocoa in the Salvation Army canteen with meals in Carlisle at night when we could afford them. I remember a delicious dinner with kind neighbours: 'This is Muscovy duck,' said my hostess. 'How interesting!' I said, 'I've never eaten Muscovy duck before. I thought people kept them as pets.' 'They do,' said my hostess, 'this was Fusspot' – and a salt tear dropped into the gravy. Fusspot was delicious.

Though I had spent a great deal of my time in the kitchen as a child, and been in charge of cake-making, baking and puddings during the holidays, my father's dislike of 'fancy food' prevented my learning anything much more complicated than bread sauce (and how few people can make that!). And as my mother had been persuaded by my aunt – in the absence of my father, soldiering abroad – to bring me up as a Christian Scientist, I had only twice tasted alcohol before I went to Oxford. The first time was when my father gave me a sip of hock, when I came down to a dinner-party at dessert-time, aged about nine; the second, aged about twelve, was when his trainer gave me a glass of home-made elderberry

19

wine to cure my whooping-cough. But then at seventeen, in 1926, I went to Oxford: no more Christian-Science church, my first cigarette, my first glass of wine, my first pint of beer, *sole Véronique*, lobster *Mornay, suprème de volaille sous cloche*, Nesselrode Pudding – I was totally and utterly hooked by that lovely sin of gluttony.

Meals varied from college to college. At Trinity we were supposed to have breakfast in hall. As I was not keen on early rising, I settled for tea and fruit in my rooms. In other colleges they had breakfast in their rooms and could even give breakfast parties. These were very agreeable: the eggs, bacon, sausages, kidneys were put down in front of a blazing fire. One started fairly late and by the time one had consumed a large breakfast with lots of coffee and marmalade it was time for the first pint of beer of the day: breakfast continued until it was time to think about luncheon.

Dons, of course, were allowed to have breakfast parties in their rooms. The President was much too civilised to do so, and the only one who ever invited me was the Dean. I had luckily been warned beforehand that, after breakfast, the guests were taken into a small unfurnished room next door to his sitting-room where they were obliged to play a special game of hockey of his invention. I kept one eye on my host and the other on the clock and when I saw a danger signal I excused myself on the grounds that I had to go to mass at Pusey House. It was not for two years that I found out how I had disgraced myself. The conversation had turned to funny books and we talked of Wodehouse, Saki, W. W. Jacobs. I said I thought Aldous Huxley so funny and quoted, as an example, that poem in *Antic Hay*:

> Christlike in my behaviour
> Like every good believer
> I imitate my Saviour
> And cultivate a beaver.

It does not strike me as very funny now.

A year later my parents were sent for, as my scout had sneaked that I kept a drawer full of unpaid bills (keeping them showed at least good intentions). He had also reported on the contents of my drink cupboard, which was always well stocked, as I was a hospitable chap, and included the ingredients for making mulled claret. Another year passed and the cox of our college boat sneaked that he had seen me at a party at the Randolph, given by two 'gay' Hungarian barons (what was *he* doing there, anyway?). I assured the Dean that I was perfectly capable of protecting myself from the advances of Hungarian barons – neither of them, rather humiliatingly, had, in fact, advanced. 'You've no moral standards,' said the trembling Dean: 'that's what comes of reading Aldous Huxley and drinking apricot brandy.'

Sunday breakfast parties at the Randolph were a great feature, mostly with people who had gone down the year before and were back for the weekend. They would begin late and end about twelve, when it would be time to cross Beaumont Street to Gug's. This exceptional don, the Taylorian Reader in Spanish, 'received' each Sunday morning. There was always a moment of anxiety as one went in as to whether one would be given sherry or marsala. Sometimes, if one had made too much noise singing John Betjeman's *D'ye ken Kolkhorst with his arty-crafty parlour?* the second glass might be marsala, to put one in one's place.

Oxford breakfasts were just a shadow of country-house breakfasts. Even in a small house such as ours there was always porridge; if there were fishcakes or kedgeree there were also boiled eggs; if there had been game the day before there would be cold partridge or pheasant; if not, cold ham or tongue. On some mornings, if my father had shot some snipe, that was the greatest treat of all. Cereals were just coming in and much despised by my father because my Aunt Laura, the great Christian Scientist, was much addicted to them: 'shredded bromo' he used to call one of them.

Later, from 1934 to 1939, I was private secretary to Christopher Turnor, who had a vast Victorian house in Lincolnshire, and there we really had breakfasts. There was porridge for those who liked it. Mrs Turnor had cereals. On Sundays he made waffles (with maple syrup and pats of butter *à part*). There were eggs for boiling and a little saucepan of hot water. There were fried or scrambled eggs, bacon, fishcakes or kedgeree, sometimes mushrooms, sometimes kidneys. There was a cold ham, Bradenham or Virginia. Cold game in season, sometimes a *terrine* of pheasant. There were home-made scones, a wholemeal loaf, toast; tea and coffee, of course; honey in a comb, one or two kinds of Women's Institute jam, marmalade. In season there were grapefruit from Florida and sometimes pommeloes; from the garden, strawberries, raspberries, gooseberries, currants; from the hot-house, peaches, nectarines and grapes. A brisk walk to church and a brisk walk back, and we were ready for a four-course luncheon.

As for luncheon at Oxford: if you were alone, you had 'beer and commons' – a pint of draught beer, a roll and a chunk of Cheddar cheese. But if you wanted to entertain, luncheon was the

ABOVE: Masie Gay and Douglas Byng in *This Year of Grace*
BELOW: 'Hutch' NOT playing the piano

time to do it – one was even allowed women guests, the thin end of the permissive wedge. I would go to the kitchen the day before and discuss with Mr Eyles, the chef, what we should have. In the winter it was usually game; in the summer, salmon. There might be lobster, hot or cold, or braised York ham, a speciality. There was Trinity Salad, which consisted of cos lettuce dressed with a mixture of spring onions; grated Cheddar; olive oil; Orleans, garlic and tarragon vinegars; with salt and pepper. In summer there was a special pudding, called (God knows why) Rodeo Pudding: bananas, raspberries and whipped cream.

It was not until the summer of 1927 that I really learnt about London. I stayed with John Hill, the decorator, and he took me to the Ivy. A rich lady who was rather keen on me took me for the first time to the Berkeley and, not knowing the geography, I followed her into the Ladies: I can laugh at it now but then I felt more like crying with shame and fleeing from the building. However, I soon became, as we all were, adopted by Ferraro and could sit for an hour in the foyer over a White Lady or a Sidecar (costing 1s 6d), waiting to see if Brian Howard or Eddie Gathorne-Hardy, Elizabeth Ponsonby or Babe Plunkett-Green came in. I could choose anything from the menu and still pay 8s 6d, the price of the set luncheon. I didn't, as others did, sign the bill. Just before the Berkeley shut last year, I lunched there with Alan Pryce-Jones. We had White Ladies for old time's sake (and how good they were!). Alan remembered how Ferraro had once said to him: 'Don't think I'm worried, Mr Pryce-Jones, but wouldn't it be more sensible to pay now? It must be so boring to pay for food you've eaten four years ago.'

Nineteen-twenty-seven was the year that the Diaghileff ballet was at Prince's Theatre and Cochran's *This Year of Grace* at the London Pavilion. Hutch played the piano in the Cochran orchestra – you could shake hands with him from the stage box (right) and go on afterwards to Chez Victor to hear him sing *Let's Fall in Love*. It was the year of the Sailor Party, the Bathing Party (at St George's Baths), the Come as Somebody Else Party. Miss Bankhead and Tom Douglas were at all of them; Lifar and June (never together) at some of them. White Ladies, Sidecars or Alexandras at the Berkeley the next day, then *œufs en cocotte à la crème, agneau de Pauillac, petits suisses* with Bar-le-Duc jam, *fraises des bois*. I don't think our wine-drinking was very sophisticated, but the kummel was served iced or *frappé* and the dear little waiter, Louis, who looked after the back room where you didn't

ABOVE: Picasso's front curtain for *Le Train Bleu,* sold in 1968 for £69,000

BELOW: Part of an old menu from *Le Jardin des Gourmets*

Poissons

Truite Saumonée froide 3/6   Saumon grillé 1er Beurnaise 3/
Turbot Véron 3/.   Maquereau Maître d'hôtel 4/
Merlun frit 1er Cajtare 4/.   Truite Amandine 4/.
      Sole frite grillée ou meunière 3/-

Plat du Jour

Chateaubriand Paluse 3/6   Escalope de Veau Zingara 3/-
Côtes d'agneau vert prés 3/.   Truite Beaunaise purée 0 frites 3/
Pilaw de foie de volaille 3/.   Kébab à l'Orientale 3/
Coq au vin de Chisitourgue 3/6   Émincé de volaille au gratin 3/.

Grillades, Viandes Froides

      Poulet de grain grillé à l'américaine 8/6
Fricassée de poulet froide 3/6   Poulet Bourguignonne froid 3/6
      Terrine Maison 3/6

have to change in the evening, made delicious *café diablé* – sugar, coffee beans, cloves, cinnamon, *flambés* in brandy, hot coffee added and strained into cups.

It was at about this time that the good restaurants began. Hitherto, there had been the hotel restaurants, of which the Savoy and the Berkeley were the best (the May Fair, where I did my training, was excellent but never fashionable), and the Soho restaurants which were cheap and amusing, but not *chic*. Boulestin was, I suppose, the pioneer but I regarded it as so serious, gastronomically, that I thought of it as a dinner restaurant and one to which I could not afford to go, unless taken. Of Boulestin more later. I cannot remember where Bellometti was – was it Lisle Street? Later he went to Leicester Square. The food was very good and, though one could not go without a tie, one could go without a hat. Grander was Sovrani in Jermyn Street, opposite the top of Bury Street. Sovrani had been *maître d'hôtel* in the Savoy Restaurant and really knew how a restaurant should be run. Breaking away from him some years later, Quaglino opened in Bury Street a few yards away. He is supposed to have said to the (then) Prince of Wales: 'Sovrani he focker my wife, I focker his business' – and he did. In 1932 Dertu and Silvy broke away from Boulestin – though not for the same reason – and opened the Jardin des Gourmets in Greek Street. It looks almost exactly the same now as it looked then, when it offered Boulestin food at prices that even I could afford.

It might be supposed that, after the breakfasts and luncheons I have described, there would be little need of tea. Necessary or not, tea in Oxford was served in one's room and usually consisted of a hot dish – buttered toast, anchovy toast, muffins, crumpets or tea-cake. If one had guests, one bought a Fuller's walnut cake. In private houses, the minimum expected was a hot dish – silver with a lid, sitting on a china bowl of hot water – thin white bread-and-butter, possibly a wholemeal loaf, a plum cake, an iced cake, a plate of macaroons. The late Lord Macclesfield used always to have bantams' eggs in small silver egg-cups. After hunting or shooting there were always boiled eggs. A Scottish peer, still with us, used always to have dripping and spring onions at tea. As a child one had always been told by one's nanny to have 'a piece of bread-and-butter to begin with' and 'a piece of bread-and-butter to finish up with' and, until the war, I felt quite guilty if I said I'd just like a small piece of Christmas cake, a barbarian if I said I'd have nothing, a rebel if I asked for a whisky-and-soda. Ivy Compton-

Burnett kept up the pre-war tea standards, with sometimes potted shrimps or Gentleman's Relish, always at least two kinds of jam and two kinds of cake, until her death last year.

Coming now to dinner: at Trinity we could not have dinner in our rooms; dinner was in hall and you paid for it three nights a week (I think) whether you had it or not. Dinner consisted always of soup, fish, meat and either savoury or pudding. I cannot recall that we ever had wine – did we at bump-suppers? We drank tankards (silver, of course) of beer. Eccentrics could, I think, have cider. If you arrived late, mentioned a woman's name, or committed some other impropriety, you were 'sconced'. That meant that a lidded silver tankard, holding two and a half pints, was brought to you by a manservant. If you downed it, without ever tipping the tankard back, the rest of the table paid for it; if you gave up before the end, the tankard circulated, everyone had a slug and you paid. I never paid.

Dining with our President, Mr Blakiston, was considered by some of my contemporaries an ordeal. I adored it. We assembled in his sitting-room, hung with Zoffanys and other eighteenth-century painters and family miniatures, and stood around drinking sherry till dinner was announced. Then we went into the dining-room and had soup, fish, *entrée*, roast, pudding, savoury, fruit, with a different wine to accompany each course.

Back into the drawing-room for more port, and one could draw him out about the Zoffanys and what members of his family they represented. That embarrassing moment of how to get away did not seem to occur: a clock struck or something, and we were shaking hands and hurrying out to shout 'Bloody Balliol, bring out your white man', to our neighbours.

In those days, undergraduates with motors were made to have a small square green lamp on the windscreen and were not supposed to go more than five miles from Oxford. Expeditions to the Bell at Hurley, the Hôtel de Paris at Bray, the Spread Eagle at Thame depended on visitors with their own motors, on hiring a huge Daimler from Mac's garage, next to the Randolph, or just breaking the rules. The Hôtel de Paris was, I suppose, the most glamorous, with shingled girls in bead dresses and their escorts in co-respondent shoes, down from London in their Isottas, electric canoes on the river and rather ordinary expensive food at London prices. The Bell looked even more dashing – it was there I first tasted Pimm's. But the Spread Eagle at Thame was presided over by that great eccentric John Fothergill, Oscar Wilde's 'architect of the moon', really the pioneer of good food in country pubs. His cookery book, alas! was written in 1943 and more about wartime cookery than about the food he produced in the 1920s. He gathered ingredients from all over the place: Hymettus honey, rose-petal jam, Toheroa soup, black beans for his special black soup, mavrodaphne for what we used to call his 'hermaphrodite trifle'. I first tasted Châteauneuf du Pape – then little known in England – at the Spread Eagle. If he liked you, you got a glass of his special liqueur after dinner – was it *centerbi*? He would never reveal. And if his wife liked you – even rarer – you got one of her special peppermints. The Spread Eagle was also wonderful for Sunday luncheons, arriving about two o'clock after a breakfast-party and a drink-party. He was a great gardener and wrote the most beautiful italic script before it became fashionable. A sweet man. I followed him to the Royal at Ascot and the Three Swans at Market Harborough. 'Robin McDouall, Lady Enid Turnor and four other Grantham greedies', he wrote in *Confessions of an Innkeeper*, 'came to luncheon yesterday.' In the loo there he had the notice (in his beautiful script): 'We aim to please. You aim, too, please.'

When we went out of college into 'digs' we could, in most, have dinner at home. I seldom did, unless I had a birthday-party or some celebration. One of the best cook-landladies was Mrs Sheppard in St John Street. Mark Ogilvie-Grant lived there my first year; later Wyndham Goodden. Her great speciality she called Lobster Cardinal Howard. I suppose a former lodger had given her the recipe for *Homard Cardinal*. By whatever name, it was delicious.

Returning to London, it was surprising how little impact the upper-class writers – Mrs Ross, Lady Harriet St Clair, Mrs Allhusen, Lady Clark of Tillyprony, Lady Jekyll – had made on private-house food. The swing away from Victorian vulgarity, initiated by Rosa Lewis, had achieved something: there was no longer rich course after rich course. Dinners were simple – and, my God! they were simple. Clear soup, fillets of sole rolled up and cooked in some nameless sauce, overcooked lamb cutlets, reclining on a mound of mashed potatoes, fruit salad and a savoury of prunes wrapped in bacon. This was the stock preliminary to a dance where there was salmon and stuffed quails – and rather good devilled bones, if you could stay the course till 2am or after. Mrs Guinness and Mrs Maugham were the pioneers of kedgeree for supper.

Dinner in restaurants had, however, become exceedingly good. Frozen food did not exist, and the Savoy and Berkeley ordered most of their meat, poultry, fruit and vegetables from Paris.

(Dinner at the Berkeley was 12s 6d – the Savoy more expensive because of the cabaret.) For serious eating there was nowhere to beat Boulestin in that supremely elegant restaurant, decorated by Marie Laurençin. The *foie gras chaud aux raisins*, the *coulibiac*, the *suprème de volaille sous cloche* were in a class by themselves. The *foie gras en croûte* at the Savoy, the *grenouilles*, the *agneau de Pauillac*, the real quails, the real *pigeons de Bordeaux*, the real Muscat grapes, were as good as you could get in Paris. There were the little touches in the service that do not exist now: the footstool for the lady, the *rinse-doigts* coming automatically, without having to be asked for. You couldn't buy a packet of Virginia cigarettes, but the attentive waiter might have one in his tailcoat pocket.

The Savoy Grill was more for me than the restaurant, particularly after the theatre – for we ate breakfast, luncheon, tea, dinner AND supper. My favourite dishes were *Tasse de Prince des Galles* – turtle soup with a pig of grapefruit, enriched with a *liaison* of egg-yolk and cream; omelette Arnold Bennett (with haddock); haddock Colbert or Monte Carlo; *suprème de volaille Jeannette*.

Looking at an old Savoy Grill menu for 1931, I quote some of the prices: *foie gras*, oysters or caviar 5s; consommé 1s 6d; most fish 3s, but *homard thermidor* 6s; partridge 12s 6d – very expensive; snipe 6s; most grills 3s 6d; most vegetables 2s 6d; most puddings 3s. But carafe wines only 3s 6d. So they were at Boulestin, where an Haut Brion 1911 was only 12s 6d and few wines more than 14s 6d. An exception was Yquem 1921 at 21s. Champagne was about the same.

What did we drink? Latish in the mornings I might drink a Tolly at home. My friend, George Harwood, who had the best set of rooms in Tom Quad, used sometimes to have sherbet parties

ABOVE: Boulestin's original letter heading by Labourer, still in use today.

ABOVE: The Savoy Orpheans in about 1927

BELOW: The interior of Boulestin's today, very largely unchanged

about midday. Before luncheon parties we would have a glass of not very dry sherry; Desmond Ryan in Balliol found some very good old Madeira. Alan Pryce-Jones (Magdalen) invented two very disgusting drinks: Phosferine in sherry and avocaat with cherry brandy. I suspect that at luncheon in my early days I had a Graves. But then I met my first wine *guru*, Mr Badge of James Brown in Ship Street (my present *guru* is Ronald Avery), who would enquire what I was having to eat and prescribe what was best to go with it. So I began to get on to dryish hock and white burgundies with fish, and red burgundies with game or meat – claret came into my life much later. My other great friend in Magdalen, Gerry Beach, discovered the college's Yquem 1911, and its Imperial Tokay from the cellars of the Emperor Franz Josef. Together we polished them off.* I don't think I ever drank port: my father's dictum – I was not then on very good terms with him – 'All wine would be port if it could', rather turned me against it.

My cousin, Bob Coe,† had had the first cocktail-shaker in Oxford. He went down just before I came up and bequeathed it to another cousin, Henry Rogers III. It was a vast thing, nearly two feet high. Henry used to pour in a bottle of gin, then add Cointreau, lemon-juice, grenadine and ice. He had an account with the Magdalen J.C.R., never having discovered that he was supposed to be a member of Wadham. I bought a smaller shaker and used to make similar concoctions – I never met a dry martini until after the last war.

At dinner, we had beer in hall, champagne cocktails at the George – or sometimes Pilsener or Münchener. After dinner, we had gin fizzes, such as I had learnt on my first visit to Paris. We seldom had a lot of beer – which I should have liked – because we were not, in those days, allowed into pubs and, when I lived in college, I was too shy to go into the J.C.R.

I see that I have left out two important places: the Eiffel Tower and the Cavendish. The Eiffel was where the White Tower is now. Its heyday was slightly before my time, the days of *The Green Hat*: Michael Arlen, Augustus John, Diana Cooper, Nancy Cunard were its stars. There was a room decorated by Wyndham Lewis in

* *In January 1941 I was lunching in Magdalen and was taken after luncheon to the J.C.R. 'What would you like?' asked my host. 'What have you got?' I stupidly replied. 'Anything you like.' Trying to be difficult, I said: 'A glass of Strega.' I got it.*

† *Robert Coe, former American Ambassador in Copenhagen.*

Vorticist style. Stulik, the *patron*, was past his prime by the time I got to know him, and his wife had become altogether too Strindbergian. Nevertheless, his *bécasse flambée* was a poem and, when the whitebait ran out, it was a joy to see him cutting up sole with a pair of rusty nail-scissors.

The Cavendish and Rosa Lewis have been well described by Daphne Fielding in *The Duchess of Jermyn Street*. She gets one of my stories slightly wrong. Staying there in about 1936, I asked for my bill, my luggage to be brought down, and my car to be brought round. I was given a bill for some £16. I protested that I had stayed only one night, had had one glass of sherry before going out to dinner and bacon and eggs in the morning. 'Think of all the free champagne you've 'ad in the past,' said Rosa. I thought, and was suitably grateful to the numerous unknown Americans who had had it on their bills. Then I realised that I was getting old; I was twenty-eight; I was expected to pay.

EDMUND PENNING-ROWSELL

An Old Champagn

THE COMITÉ
Interprofessionel du Vin de Champagne,
in Epernay, tell me that there are no fewer than 144 champagne
houses; this in addition to the 2000 growers who make and sell
their own champagne, and the vast number of *marques* or trade
names owned by merchants.

Of this gross of 'maisons', not more than a handful have an international reputation, based on substantial and usually very old
connections in various foreign countries. A house well known in one
export market may be unknown elsewhere. However, in these days
one would be ill-advised to judge the quality of any wine by the
size of the firm that makes or sells it. Accordingly, on a recent visit
to Champagne I asked the C.I.V.C. to give me introductions to
some of the smaller houses outside the group of *grandes marques* – a
somewhat arbitrary 'club' of shippers particularly associated with
export to Britain, the largest foreign market for champagne.

Among these smaller houses was Deutz and Geldermann at Ay,
a few miles upstream from Epernay in the Marne valley. The head-
quarters of several well-known champagne houses, Ay looks across
the river and the tree-lined Marne-Rhine canal to the Côte des
Blancs, the source of the best white wines for the normal blends of
black and white grapes that constitute a champagne *cuvée*. Ay, like
many wine villages in France, hides its charms and its champagne
activities behind high walls, and Deutz and Geldermann, in a small
lane lying back from the main street, is no exception. Within a

courtyard adorned by oleanders and pomegranate trees growing in champagne barrels (taken indoors in the winter) is a charming two-storey house, part dating back to the early eighteenth century. This occupies two sides of the Cour d'Honneur, and the third contains such surface buildings as offices, despatch department, and the like, which partly cover the three or four kilometres of subterranean cellars. These are on two levels, and the upper one is finely brick-lined.

The house of Deutz and Geldermann was founded in 1838, at a time when a number of other celebrated champagne houses opened their doors and began to dig their cellars. Pommery was founded in 1836, Krug in 1843 and Pol Roger in 1849. This was a time when the French economy was expanding, and Louis Philippe's minister, Guizot, made his famous exhortation to his countrymen, *'Enrichissez-vous!'* That quite a number of French people were unable to take advantage of this encouraging advice may be shown by the subsequent downfall of Guizot's master in the 1848 Revolution, but for the fortunate bourgeoisie this was a time when life was good and champagne an obvious adjunct to good living.

However, on the whole, then and for many years to come, the champagne trade was basically an export one, and it was largely directed by people of foreign origin, notably Germans. Both William Deutz and Pierre Hubert Geldermann were born in Aachen (Aix-la-Chapelle), in 1809 and 1811 respectively, although the Geldermann family originally came from the Netherlands. The Bollingers,

35

These engravings of Deutz and Geldermann's cellars at Ay appeared in the Golden Book of London c. 1870.
ABOVE: Excavating new cellars at Ay.
OPPOSITE: Drawing off the *cuvée* at Deutz and Geldermann's.

the Heidsiecks, the Krugs and the Mumms also all came from Germany. This may be attributed not only to the proximity of Germany to Rheims and Epernay, but also to the development of the *sekt* industry in Germany; in those days, of course, *sekt* was not made in tanks as most of it is today, but by the *méthode champenoise:* fermentation in bottle.

Deutz and Geldermann is still a family firm in the sense that it is run and owned by the descendants of the founders. William Deutz died in 1884, having been predeceased by Pierre Gelderman by a dozen years. The latter's son, Alfred Pierre, married William Deutz's daughter, sister of René William Deutz; the two sons ran the business until their deaths in 1908 and 1897 respectively. Then René Francois Lallier, who had married René Deutz's daughter, headed the house in 1904, and after the death of the younger Geldermann ran the firm until his death in 1938, when he was succeeded by the present chairman, his son Jean Lallier. The latter's son André is now managing director. To complete the family picture, Alfred Geldermann's daughter married Charles van Cassel, who took over his father-in-law's share of the firm, but when he died in 1919 the Lallier branch took over the concern, although Mme van Cassel died only as recently as 1966.

In one wing of the old house her apartments remain largely unaltered, furnished in the Second Empire style. Heavy with red and gold, with tightly buttoned, closely upholstered furniture and weighty family portraits, these rooms are charmingly nostalgic or severely claustrophobic according to taste. Certainly they recall a period when Deutz champagne was prospering. Thereafter the business continued to expand and reached its peak for many years in the pre-1914 period.

As already mentioned, champagne was largely an export trade. At the beginning of the century three bottles were sold abroad for every one consumed at home, and although domestic demand rose sharply thereafter, even on the eve of the First World War nearly 21 million bottles were exported out of total sales of 30 million. In this trade Deutz and Geldermann had a secure place, concentrating on the British, German and Russian markets. This last was not numerically so important as the first two, but they shipped a good deal of sweet (*doux*) champagne to sweet-toothed Russian grand dukes and rich businessmen. How considerable was the sweetness may be gauged by the fact that Imperial Russia demanded a *dosage* of twelve per cent liqueuring, compared with one to one-and-a-quarter for the Deutz *brut* of today.

Just before the First World War the firm was shipping over 200,000 bottles to Britain, a total that would be envied today by many of the *grandes marques*. In a 1909 list of the International Exhibition Co-operative Wine Society, Deutz and Geldermann's Gold Lack Extra Dry 1904 was offered at 78s a dozen – 11½d less than to-day's customs duty on a single bottle. The non-vintage Cabinet was listed at 68s 6d. The vintage wine sold at the same price as Pol Roger and Charles Heidsieck, while Krug, Bollinger and Ruinart were 2s a case and Roederer 4s a case dearer.

Two years later, the firm suffered in the celebrated 'Revolt of the Vignerons' of April 1911. Times had been terribly hard for the growers, who were incensed at the action of those firms in Epernay that bought cheap white wines from the Loire as the basis of their 'champagne'. Assembling in the Marne Valley, they were unable to reach Epernay, which was heavily guarded by troops and police. Thereupon they vented their grievances elsewhere on champagne houses guiltless of importing grapes. These included Ayala and Deutz and Geldermann at Ay. The latter suffered extensive damage: the surface buildings were all burnt, and the interior gutted. Although the cellars were spared, all the young wine in cask was impregnated with smoke; some of the casks were damaged by fire; and a good many bottles were stolen. Although the champagne houses were insured, it took them a long time to recover, and then came the First World War as a further disaster for the whole trade.

So, after the war, Deutz turned more to the French market, and although today they export forty per cent of the 400,000 bottles they sell annually – with Italy as their biggest foreign customer – they are probably better known within France. Thirty per cent of their domestic business is direct to private customers.

One of the distinctions between champagne houses is whether or not they own vineyards. For the first forty years or so of this century the champagne trade was usually so depressed that the ownership of vineyards was a very doubtful proposition. The price of grapes was low, and it was more profitable to buy them in the open market. To this day a number of such well-known houses as Charles Heidsieck and Krug own no vineyards. Others, like Bollinger, Pommery and Deutz, are proprietors, and this is of great importance now that demand for grapes exceeds supply.

Considering their moderate size, Deutz are considerable vineyard owners, and their 30 hectares supply forty per cent of their present needs. They are dispersed along the Marne Valley, in Ay, Mareuil and Bisseuil, as well as at Pierry and Moussy just south of Epernay, and at Villeneuve near Le Mesnil on the much esteemed Côte des Blancs, where the best white grapes come from. These vineyards are in favoured sites, as may be judged by their grading. The price of champagne grapes is strictly controlled by the C.I.V.C., which has divided up the whole region into zones of quality. Ay, for example, is a 100 per cent district, but far away in the outlying Aube area, the percentage may come down to 75. The average percentage of the Deutz vineyards is 95 per cent, and in 1969 the top price for grapes was 4·85 francs per kilo. Roughly 1½ kilos are needed to produce a litre of champagne.

This is not the place to describe the production of champagne, the most complicated form of wine-making in the world, but one or two details struck me when I visited Deutz and Geldermann's cellars. First, a small matter of corks. A bottle of champagne needs two corks: the first, the *bouchon de tirage*, is applied when the young wine is bottled prior to its second fermentation; the second, the *bouchon d'expédition*, is driven in after the disgorging, when the sediment is removed and the *dosage* added. These corks have to be of very good quality, and today the first cork costs 25 centimes and the second one 40 centimes apiece. So in recent years most champagne houses have gone over to the crown cork, the *bouchon couronne*, for the first cork. (Open a bottle of champagne, and you can easily tell whether this is the case, for the crown cork requires a lip on the bottle.) It is claimed that this makes no difference, but Deutz only use it for their non-vintage wine; their vintage champagnes, including their special *blanc-de-blancs cuvée*, have large corks from the beginning. This is in line with the practice of the more traditional houses.

Secondly, the amount of time allowed after the *dégorgement* and the insertion of the new cork and before dispatch always seems to me of importance. This allows the wine and the cork to settle down, but all too often these days the newly dosed champagne is cased and sent off almost at once. True, a certain amount of 'landed-age' is usually given after arrival here in Britain, but this is uncertain in these days of capital shortage and credit squeeze. Therefore I was glad to know that Deutz and Geldermann give a minimum of three months in their cellars for their non-vintage and a year for the vintage wine.

What style of champagne does this house make? Ay wines themselves are strong and *corsé* with plenty of body, and their presence is reflected in Deutz's blends. While not so full-bodied and 'weighty' as some champagnes, they are certainly fruity and what

ABOVE: The Cour d'Honneur at Ay

PREVIOUS PAGE: Champagne awaiting maturity
FOLLOWING PAGE: The champagne riots at Ay in 1911

ABOVE: Demonstrators on the march to Troyes, April 1911
BELOW: Deutz & Geldermann's premises on fire at Ay, 1911
Picture from *Illustrated London News* 22 April 1911

might be called 'generous' wines without being sweet, and with a fruity nose. The '64 wine that I sampled on the spot was certainly quite a big wine as champagnes go. Like many shippers they have a *blanc de blancs*, sold in France and elsewhere on the Continent in a colourless bottle with the name Cuvée William Deutz. In England it is sold simply as a *blanc de blancs*. The '61 that I tasted was very elegant, an excellent aperitif champagne.

However, the wine that really impressed me, as a lover of old champagne, was the 1949 in magnum, served at dinner with the family. Disgorged about four years previously, this 20-year-old wine was still very pale in colour, firm, with plenty of character and no sign of age. Only a very well-made, well-balanced champagne will show as freshly as this one did.

Snakes Chop Suey

T HOME I NEVER HAVE trouble in Chinese restaurants but here in Fook Tsun Street in Hong Kong's Kowloon peninsula it was like beginning again from scratch. 'What would you like as a starter?' I glanced uneasily at the list of soups. Everything was unfamiliar. 'Lo Po Nui Jo T'ang; Huo Tui Pai Ts'ai; Nai Yu Hseih Jo.' And last on the list, the single word 'Sai'. It had to be something, so I finally took the plunge. 'I'll have the Sai soup,' I said – 'if only because it's shortest.' Bill (his real name was unpronounceably Chinese) leered across the table at me. 'I wouldn't say it's *shortest*. It's longer than the rest.' I decided it was a queer Chinese joke. I didn't get the point – then.

Sai soup for two was duly ordered. The waiter poured out glasses of warm rice wine and disappeared. Two minutes later he was back again with a sack firmly knotted at the top. He threw it down at my feet, produced a penknife and a small whetstone and started sharpening the blade. Bill took all this in his stride and chatted casually – a bit too casually for my liking. I already had premonitions of disaster, and these were heightened when I noticed vague squirming movements inside the sack.

The waiter knelt down, untied the sack, fumbled cautiously around the opening. Suddenly he pulled out a wriggling tail, followed by a length of thick brown snake. He kept the snake's head inside the sack, put one foot on the tail, stretched the body, grasped his penknife and slit the belly. At the end of the incision he popped

out what looked like a gland about the size of a grape. 'That's the bile duct,' said Bill helpfully. The waiter cut off the head of the snake, brought the bile duct to the table and washed it in a small bowl of water. He made a tiny nick at one end, held it over my glass and squeezed the bile drop by drop into rice wine. 'Good for rheumatism,' said Bill encouragingly. 'But I haven't got rheumatism,' I moaned. 'In that case,' he said, 'it will act as a preventative.'

I have one guiding principle on these occasions, which have cropped up in various parts of the world, and it's this: if what you're offered is a popular local dish, however peculiar, there can be no really physical harm and you might as well try it. The Sai came on the table. It was a large steaming bowl of clear soup in which five skinned snakes were only too visible. To get the worst over first, I sipped the wine . . . slightly bitter, an 'interesting' taste, rather like Fijian kava, not at all bad. The soup was quite delicious.

We were joined at coffee by a Tanzanian student on an engineering course, and the conversation turned naturally enough to strange foods. He recounted an experience of his own in Burundi, where he'd spent several months during the previous year. It appeared that meat was scarce, but in the local market the stall-holders were doing a brisk trade in rats, which the Burundis cooked with onions, tomatoes, green peppers and curry powder. The Tanzanian was naturally disgusted and preferred to eat his rice dry. But after a fortnight the plain rice was becoming monotonous and the rat stew smelled more and more inviting. The next day he tried a spoonful.

He liked it and for the rest of his stay in Burundi ate rats with relish.

What part does prejudice play in our eating habits? I thought about this on the way back to my hotel. Are we repelled by strange foods simply because they're different from what we're used to? And is any national diet, our own included, entirely free from revolting oddities? The snake-cutting episode, genuinely horrific, had somehow stirred a vague fragment of memory and now, as I walked under the frenzied neon of Kowloon's Nathan Road, it suddenly clicked into place. Eels! Years ago in my home town, watching with the ghoulish interest of a small boy, I'd seen them slit alive in exactly the same way. For all I know some other little boys may be watching still.

Looking back on my own travels, it seems there's hardly a living thing that isn't eaten by somebody, somewhere. Even the Tanzanian's rat-diet is tame compared with the daily menu of many West Africans. Lake flies, locusts, flying ants, beetles and mashed maggots are standard dishes. In the South Pacific, puppies rolled in clay and slowly baked over hot stones are a special delicacy, while an Indian village feast features monkey smothered in chilli, wrapped in plantain leaves and cooked in wood embers as the main course.

Next day Bill phoned me. I'd acquitted myself well on the snake soup. Would I like to come back to Fook Tsun Street that night and have a whole snake feast? He had to know well in advance, he told me, because the banquet would take time to prepare. I said yes and arrived with hardly any qualms. The Tanzanian was there too, and three other Chinese I hadn't met before. We started off with Ching Chung Tai Shee Keng, or 'snake kettle', a huge dish with snake meat, abalone, fish-maw, Chinese ham, orange peel and wood fungus, worked our way happily through several other delicious snake courses and finished up with So Jar Lung Fung Kuen – pancake rolls filled with fried, shredded snake meat and chicken gizzards and garnished with chrysanthemum petals and lemon leaves. It was a memorable and enjoyable meal.

This time the talk turned into a competition, with each of us trying to cap the others' food stories. One of the Chinese explained to the Tanzanian that birds' nest soup wasn't really birds' nest at all, but only the solidified spittle with which the birds stick the pieces of grass and straw together; the Tanzanian weighed in with his rat story. I told them of the Masai tribesmen in Kenya who puncture an artery in a cow's neck, draw off a calabash of blood,

48

stop the bleeding, milk the cow and then drink blood and milk together. The Chinese were so sickened they almost choked on their snake rolls.

I went on to mention the peculiarities of West African diet. 'Couldn't anything be done to stop these people eating insects and maggots?' one of the Chinese asked indignantly. 'What about UNO – don't they have any people out there?' 'Yes, they have,' I replied. 'Officials of the Food and Agriculture Organisation of the UN have been testing the food value of African diets. They find that flies, locusts and maggots have a nineteen per cent protein content, which is exactly the same as that of cows, sheep, pigs and elephants. Since protein is so scarce in Africa, the FAO people encourage pastoral tribes to stick to their insect diet. Fly-protein is better than no protein at all.'

I still had a trump card up my sleeve. 'Have any of you heard of the South Sea Islanders who starve a pig for a week and then give it a banquet of tender veal . . .?' Bill pressed me to continue. 'Two hours later they slaughter the pig and remove and cook the stomach, which is stuffed to bursting point with soft, half-digested meat.'

'I've heard of another tribe with a similar custom,' said Bill quietly. 'They don't feed the animal before slaughter but they stuff the empty stomach with all sorts of chopped entrails. Pretty disgusting. I think they call it haggis.'

I hastily turned the conversation to oysters. I'd just flown in from Sydney, where the oysters are half the size of Whitstable's but unspeakably delicious. Some chance remark of mine suddenly made the rat-eating Tanzanian sit up and take notice. 'But surely you don't swallow them *alive*? Good God!'

They all chewed their snake in shocked silence.

ALAN BRIEN

Strictly from Hunger

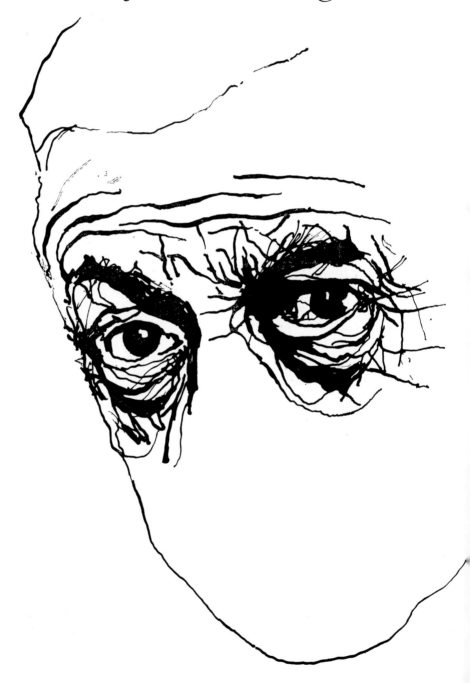

RE YOU SURE you won't stay for some cawfee?' the Duke of Windsor asked me. It was like one of those anxiety dreams. Only he was the one in the pyjamas, and there I was, un- shaven and dishevelled, backing towards the door, and already I could feel the house detectives of the Waldorf-Towers on their way up to beat the daylights out of me, and there was Lord Beaverbrook in some other suite, pacing Napoleonically up and down, dictating a memo firing me for more than usual unpunctuality. I wish now that I had taken the line that the invitation of a Royal Duke over- rides the summons of a Canadian baron. His Royal Highness looked as if he might have been glad of the company and I would have been left with an anecdote of less awkward length. But, in the circumstances, all I could think of was a speedy escape.

The circumstances were these. I had been woken in my bed at the Gladstone Hotel in 1957 by a message that my employer, Lord Beaverbrook, wished to see me now, if not sooner, on a matter of extreme importance. I slapped on a minimum of clothes with all the elegance of a scarecrow, knowing that I could attend to my fly buttons, laces, tie and hair in the Waldorf-Towers lift. The lift was not more automatic than I was – without hesitation, I stopped at the usual floor and hurled myself at the usual door.

It did seem a bit odd that there was a black major-domo, but stranger people had been hired for stranger jobs on Beaverbrook

Newspapers. After all, my boss was the Empire Crusader and had presumably just flown in from Jamaica or the Bahamas. I pushed the man aside shouting 'Lord Beaverbrook – urgent' and made for the domestic section of the apartment. I had been conditioned not to hang about standing on ceremony but to present myself, clean and bright (and slightly oiled) like a guardsman's rifle, even within reach of the shower's overspill. It seemed even odder that a familiar stranger should appear at the bedroom door in pyjamas of enormous stripe and ghastly hue.

I recognised the face in one and a half seconds, with its pinky-brown, lined surface like a foot that has been in the bath too long. The Duke of Windsor! But I still thought he might have been put up for the night by the most loyal of his old champions. 'Lord Beaverbrook – urgent,' I said. 'Max?' asked the Duke. 'Is he here?' I began to run out of steam but clung to the only certainty in a collapsing world. 'But I thought he was always here,' I piped. 'I mean when he's here, he always stays *here*, here.' The Duke considered this with regal calm. After a while, he replied 'I don't think he's ever *here* when *I'm* here.'

At last, as in a Raymond Chandler story, all the pieces of the jigsaw fell into place. I began backing towards the door. 'Are you sure you won't stay for some cawfee?' the Duke of Windsor asked me. Only later did it occur to me that the ex-King's English was no longer the Queen's English and that he pronounced 'coffee' as 'cawfee'. Only now does it occur to me that American cawfee is an entirely different beverage from English, or French, or Turkish, coffee. It deserves an intonation all of its own.

I was brought up on coffee as a thick, black, viscous liquid in a bottle that was then mixed with boiling water and evaporated milk. I hated it for its sweet, tinny, burnt flavour, like caramelised soy sauce. At Oxford, in the middle of the war, coffee was so little regarded that it was never rationed. Despite the blockading U-boats, and the shortage of foreign currency, the brown beans arrived in the shops every week, even if nothing else did. I was introduced to coffee, middle-class style. The university was full of men who ignored the topics on which I could speak – sex, beer and politics – but talked only of coffee, and occasionally bridge. Every one of them had his own coffee ritual – some ground it themselves, some even roasted it, almost all bought it at dawn and brewed it the same day, in saucepans (paying great attention to tapping the side with a spoon), in metal jugs, in glass flasks, passed along tubes, strained through filters, in individual cups or in huge carboys. It always smelled better than it tasted, and to me it always tasted bitter, cloudy, teeth-gritting and throat-coating.

In the R.A.F. we got coffee mass-production style. It was simply one of three names, chosen at random, to describe a scalding, ersatz, lead-poisoned flow from a paint-peeling boiler. There were those who claimed to be able to differentiate various flavours in this metallic seepage, arguing that 'coffee' was what looked like tea and reeked of cocoa, but I never graduated to such penitentiary connoisseurship.

Since then, I have tried the best French coffee, which still affects me like a mixture of gravy and quinine with a hint of ear wax. I have tried the best Turkish, which is Euphrates mud sprinkled with broken glass and crystallised fudge. But the only coffee which lives up to its commercials is American cawfee.

Until I went to America, in 1956, I could not understand how its inhabitants could regard the stuff as a substitute for breakfast. But it *is* a breakfast, a creamy, mild, healthful restorative which is actually a pleasure to gulp. It is also elevenses, lunch, tea and supper, a transfusion that you can feel working instantly in the veins. It is best – or perhaps I only tasted it there first – in a diner, especially one of those aluminium-ribbed caravans by the highway which somehow seem to embody all the fantasied delights of your ideal eating-place on wheels, though they never move. But cawfee is obtainable as the square's fix, the drug of the innocents, almost anywhere in an American city. I used to resent the insistent American complaint that abroad there was 'no decent cawfee'. Now I know they are right. I only wish they could teach us how to make it.

Cawfee is a meal. All genuine American meals attempt to provide enough nourishment for at least a day. They are prepared on the assumption that consumers are heroic backwoodsmen, fresh into town from splitting rails, rolling logs or rounding up strays. Sophisticated Europeans tend to scoff at these wineless, carbohydrate-piled meals centred around bloody haunches of meat. But if you are hungry, and cannot afford a siesta, American food is probably the cheapest and most satisfying in the world. Only there can I really enjoy steak. Despite the deep-freeze and the hormone injections, the deeply held faith that quality is a by-product of quantity, the ordinary, average American steak-house provides a steak which arouses the carnivore in all of us. You know you are consuming part of a once-living animal – not the leather-sealed sliver of biltong you find in cheap restaurants in Britain, where the natives prefer it fried, or the slippery, mushy strands of grey delicacy buried under cream sauces they adore in France.

I am not talking of the French or Italian or German or Chinese restaurants in America. (Though it is worth noting that Britons who boast that they always eat the food of any country they visit, and who would rather starve than order fish-and-chips in Genoa or a nice cup of tea in Marseilles, break their rules in America where they seek out exactly the kind of restaurants they patronise in Soho.) American food pretends to be the sustenance of the he-man. It might be more accurate to describe it as the favourite nosh of the international adolescent.

It has the conservatism, and conventionality, that lurks under the nonconformist uniform of youngsters everywhere. It is suspicious of all secret, hidden entrails – liver, kidneys, sweetbreads, brains, bone marrow. It rejects, no matter how WASP the community, whatever might appear not quite *kosher* – rabbit, hare, kid, snails, frog legs, even mutton except as lamb cutlets. Among mammals, beef is king, and the monarch is sacrificed and devoured in amounts that would astonish even Sir James George Frazer of *The Golden Bough*. Their hamburgers are to our mince what Roman *pasta* is to our tinned spaghetti.

Shellfish are as various and inviting as the meat is standard and safe. Though scattered across an enormous continent, Americans live in a continual concern about sea food which our small island never matches. Soft-shelled crabs, downed like whitebait, carapace and all, are only one of the delicacies unknown to most Europeans. Quite unpretentious people, with no posing as gourmets, know the seasons of fish and the times to eat them at their peak. They also have game, at home and in restaurants, beyond any British expectation.

American food seems designed to entice the appetites of sluggish teenagers who resist plain vegetables simply served. An enormous number of recipes and local dishes concentrate on mixing flavours, blending savoury and sweet, pungent and bland, as, for example, in barbecue sauces for spareribs. There are also beetroots with orange dressing; red cabbage with apples; white cabbage with vinegar, sugar and egg yolks; tomatoes stuffed with cream cheese and walnuts; Boston baked beans with fat bacon, sugar and black treacle. Thousand Island dressing usually replaces mayonnaise (how often do we find *that* here, except in *Good Food Guide* places?) with orange and lemon juice added to olive oil.

American food is pioneer food, workers' food, God's guarantee that the Depression will never come again, so long as you finish your Baked Alaska or your Floating Island. To those who want small, subtle meals, with a hint of decadence, accompanied by wine, twice a day, the American menu grows stultifying, and fattening (don't forget all those pies and fritters and popovers and ice creams). I must confess that in New York, after a token debauch, I return to my favourite French and Italian restaurants, which are much the same as in London. But for popular catering, giving the man-on-the-sidewalk what he wants, America is way ahead of Britain in quality, cleanliness, efficiency and value for money. And there is always the cawfee.

DERMOT MORRAH

Mint Jule

WHEN I WENT UP TO
New College, the story was that
we owed our first acquaintance with mint julep to the War Between
the States. A young Confederate officer on leave had dined one
night in hall as the guest of an undergraduate, and been overjoyed
to find with what general sympathy the Southern cause was then
regarded in the college. But he was distressed to find that they could
not drink a mint julep to the confusion of Abe Lincoln, because his
hosts had never heard of his national drink. So, in gratitude for the
high principles of his young hosts, he proceeded to endow mint
julep. He presented the college with a handsome silver cup, and
with it a sufficient capital sum to provide mint julep for everyone
in hall on each first of June, being the anniversary of the night he
dined. In return he asked only that a place should be laid for him at
the senior scholars' table, where he had sat, in case he should
unexpectedly turn up.

This was the tradition duly passed down to me on the first Mint
Julep Night I enjoyed, 1 June, 1919. As will appear, it was far
from accurate; but I think I can trust my memory for the procedure
observed that night. The place for the patron was duly laid, with
a scout standing over it to warn off any undergraduate who should
inadvertently try to sit there. Dinner ran its ordinary course; but
with the cheese a number of silver quart cups were carried in – for
the college numbers were now at least three times those of what we
supposed to be the date of origin of the ceremony. What I think
was the original cup was taken to the High Table for the Warden
to have the first drink. The cups then went round the tables in the
manner of a loving cup, passing from hand to hand with exchange
of bows. On receiving the cup, one observed first that its outer
surface was frosted over with cold. Its contents looked at first sight
like a small shrub; this was in fact a cluster of mint sprigs pressed

56

so tight together that one might wonder there was any room for liquid. But in fact you could push the verdure aside with your nose and draw through it a highly spirituous decoction with a distinctive flavour that I now realise was based on bourbon whisky. But it was so icy cold that the drinker withdrew gasping after one mouthful.

Such, certainly, was – and still is – the ceremony, but it was not until this year, when the Editor of *The Compleat Imbiber* asked me to give an account of it in print, that I realised how inaccurate oral tradition can be, even in a house devoted to scholarship. I wrote to ask for the blessing of the Warden, and not only did he invite me to dine at High Table on last year's Mint Julep Night, but the Domestic Bursar let me loose among the papers relating to the origin and continuation of the observance. He warned me that they were very incomplete; but I found enough to make me set aside the oral tradition I had long accepted.

Out at once, then, goes the Civil War. The true origin is nearly a quarter of a century further back, on 1 June, 1845. On that night there dined in New College a wealthy gentleman of South Carolina named (in the file) William Howard Trapier, who was on a visit to England for the first time. It is assumed that he was a graduate of the university of South Carolina.

Trapier dined as the guest of an undergraduate; but he did not sit at the senior scholars' table, for the good reason that proud New College acknowledged no such humble status. It was a close corporation of seventy members, all educated at Winchester, and all called Fellows (like the members of the daughter college of All Souls to this day). Until they graduated they were called probationer or junior fellows, and they then succeeded to full fellowships as their seniors married and departed. It was only ten years since the college had voluntarily surrendered its ancient privilege of taking all degrees without examination; so the senior dons at the

High Table that night, all of course unmarried Masters of Arts and many of them Doctors of Divinity, had arrived at their pleasant eminence by an automatic process of lapsing time, having taken only one examination in their leisurely lives, when they were elected scholars of Winchester at the age of twelve.

So William Trapier, instead of sitting with these reverend but not oppressively learned gentlemen, sat among the young laymen at the junior fellows' table in the body of the hall. As to how the subject of mint julep came up, there are divergent accounts in the college files, and I fall back on the brief account given by the Domestic Bursar to a press inquirer only four years ago, though it is only partly substantiated by the records, and I suspect that there has been some reliance on oral tradition. The Bursar writes that at the table on that first of June, Trapier 'was asked by his host what he would like to drink and asked for a mint julep. Shocked to find that this beverage was unknown to the college he gave the college his recipe and a silver cup, with the suggestion that mint julep should be drunk every year on 1 June from then on. He is alleged to have given the college some money to endow this, but we can find no trace of this, and so far as our records go there has always been a charge on battels for mint julep every year.'

This account is confirmed and supplemented by Barry Bingham, writing in the *Louisville Courier-Journal* for July 1942. He was told that the famous recipe had never been written down. It was preserved in the memory of the J.C.R. butler, who told him: 'I learned it from the dying lips of my predecessor, and I swore I would never pass it on except to the man who will some day succeed me.'

One other scrap of information comes from the J.C.R. tradition. The place laid for Trapier is set because he said that he would return one day to see that his wishes had been carried out. The college has never received any intimation of his death, so a place is kept in hall in case even now he may claim it.

The most concrete piece of evidence in the archives is the Trapier Cup itself. It is of antique silver and holds a quart. The hall marks show that it was made in England by Richard Gurney and Company in 1740. In the college inventory it is described as 'large-bellied, with double-scrolled handle (vine leaves) and embossed with scrolls and flowers; and it records its own history in the inscription: Coll B.V.M. Winton apud Oxonienses D.D. Guliel. Heyword* Trapier . . . A.S. 1845.'

In this cup, reinforced by others from the college plate as

numbers expanded, we must suppose that mint julep circulated annually for nearly a hundred years until, as will appear, the custom was allowed for a time to lapse. Apart from the American cuttings, which show that the subject was still of interest across the ocean, the college papers contain no further reference until 1956, when the late David Ogg, a senior Fellow of New College, was invited to spend a year as Visiting Professor in the University of South Carolina. The college thought that the occasion demanded some expression of its gratitude for the gift of 1845 and of respect for the donor's memory. Accordingly Ogg was asked to take with him and offer to his hosts another silver cup. A photograph of it is preserved at New College. It shows a vessel of more austere design than the Trapier cup, corresponding to the movement of taste towards greater simplicity that had gone on between 1740 and the date of its hall-mark – 1767. It is inscribed in English: 'Presented to the University of South Carolina by David Ogg, Visiting Professor 1956–7, in commemoration of a cup given in 1845 to New College by William Hayward Trapier. And in renewal of an old bond of Friendship and Esteem. MCMLVII.' On the other side of the cup are engraved the arms of William of Wykeham, now used as their own by both his colleges; the seal of the University of South Carolina; and the motto *Emollit mores nec sinit esse feros*; though whether this last refers to the civilising influence of university education or of mint julep I do not feel sure.

In spite of this late expression of gratitude, it is not at all clear that Mint Julep Night was still being celebrated. Quite recent correspondence shows that at some time or another it was allowed to lapse; and the most likely implication was that this had occurred during or in consequence of the Second World War. The correspondence was with one of the honorary fellows, an eminent Latin scholar who had graduated from New College nearly sixty years ago and had since followed a career of great distinction in another college. He was shocked to learn that mint julep was not served on the proper night in 1963, and promptly offered an anonymous gift of £250 to ensure the revival of the old custom.

* *This must be the correct spelling, though several variants appear in the documents and in this article. Trapier was the son of Benjamin Foisson Trapier and Hannah Shubrick Heyword.*

So at last Mint Julep Night came to be endowed, and the new cycle of observance was inaugurated on 1 June, 1964. How close the ceremony now is to that contemplated by William Trapier and presumably first celebrated in 1846 I dare not say. Dining last year, on the fiftieth anniversary of my first taste of mint julep, I saw at once that there had been substantial changes in my lifetime; but who am I to say that these could not have been a reversion to still older practice than I knew? I can only record what happened.

It was many years since I had dined in New College; and I was immediately startled by the presence of a number of lady guests, both at the High Table and among the undergraduates. After that I was prepared for surprises, and they began at once. The cups of mint julep appeared, not at the end of the meal, but immediately after the soup. The close-packed bush of mint had disappeared, leaving only a few loose sprigs for ornament and flavour. The mixture was agreeably iced, but not to that preternatural or Arctic degree that had taken my youthful breath away. We passed the cups round and drank standing, with ritual bows, after the manner I remembered; but then the cups were not taken away but set down on the tables and replenished at intervals. Anyone who felt like it took another drink and passed the cup on to his left-hand neighbour; and in fact the cups were almost continuously circulating from beginning to end of the meal. I did not myself think that the julep, stimulating and fortifying as it was, harmonised particularly well with the white and red wines on the High Table; so I contented myself with the first ritual draught. But several of my neighbours, and perhaps most of the undergraduates of both sexes, were plainly treating mint julep as the staple beverage of the evening; and I had tasted enough to sympathise with them. It is a fine lively drink.

And what, after all this, *is* mint julep as drunk in New College on 1 June? That remains a mystery. Whether or not it is strictly true that Trapier's recipe has never been written down, I at least have not seen it; and if I had, then as a loyal son of New College I should be scrupulous to keep the secret. The best approximation I can offer is to transcribe a recipe from our greatest living authority:

. . . Crush one lump of sugar at the bottom of a tall glass. Add half a dozen small sprigs of mint, which should first be lightly twisted between the fingers to break the skin of the leaves. Cover with whisky and allow to stand for ten minutes. Then pour in the balance of whisky (to make a long drink a full whisky glass should be used), fill the glass with finely crushed ice and stir rapidly with a spoon until the outside of the glass is frosted. Serve garnished with mint sprigs. The best Maryland juleps are made with old rye. . . .

So writes André Simon. But Maryland is neither South Carolina nor Oxford, and I know that New College uses bourbon.

N. G. B. REID*

Oysters at Jesus

NE DAY, IN THE fortieth year of the reign of Queen Victoria, newly created Empress of India, Mr E. Baddeley, commoner of Jesus College, Cambridge, was thinking of oysters. No ordinary oysters, but natives culled from the dark beds of the East Anglian coast. Not a mere dozen, but a whole barrelful. Convinced that his stomach could not possibly accommodate such a quantity, he hit upon the idea of inviting a few select friends to share the delicacies. Washed down with liberal quantities of stout, the oysters were obviously a success, for as the evening drew to a close, all agreed that the party would bear repetition at least once fortnightly.

Since that time, oysters have been consumed at more or less regular intervals in the college, by the club that arose from that first extraordinary meeting – a club restricted, as it still is, to twelve members of the college, not necessarily all of them undergraduates.

As with any club, the Natives have had their ups and downs. The seventy-fifth anniversary year saw their compulsory disbandment on the strict orders of the Senior Tutor, who could not in his official capacity approve of junketings which lasted into the small hours.

* President, 1969, The Natives Club.

So at the close of the Michaelmas Term, the Natives were to be no more.

At the first dinner of Lent term, 1962, however, twelve men stood up after grace had been read in hall, mouthed a silent toast, and then raised a mug of stout to their lips. That same night saw strange goings-on in one of the college lodging houses. Twelve begowned figures eventually made their separate entrances through the front door. Thence to a small back room, where glasses and sherry were awaiting them, and where the twelve members once again showed their colours.

A word, incidentally, about these colours, which bear no relation to the somewhat unprepossessing exterior of an oyster, being black, pale blue and pink. So violent a combination that even the normally imperturbable head porter of the Savoy has been known to blink on glimpsing them. Some weeks after this clandestine meeting, the Senior Tutor, a reasonable man, withdrew his ruling and allowed the club to revert to its former status.

At its formation, the founder members had drawn up a book of rules, prefaced by the following – 'The object of this club is for friendly reunions and social meetings.' So it remains today, though the scale of the club's activities has been necessarily tailored to suit the undergraduate pocket of the middle twentieth century. Last term we were pleased to welcome a former president back to the club for a Sunday breakfast, especially since he was equipped with a bottle of 1929 College porter. This was the legendary president who had consumed ninety-six oysters at one sitting, undoubtedly the record.

The rules have changed slightly over the past ninety years, but their spirit remains the same. One states that a fine of two shillings and sixpence shall be levied upon any member who should arrive late for a meeting, or should fail to sport the club tie. No mean feat to knot a tie of those colours when suffering from the proverbial night before. Such fines as were received were kept by the Treasurer until sufficient had accumulated to buy a piece of silver. Certainly, judging by the amount of plate now owned by the club, Natives are by tradition anything but punctual. The major item of our collection, presented by the founder members in 1877, is a delightful punch bowl (see illustration), from the depths of which many a pleasant evening must have sprung. Other pieces include a set of oyster forks, oyster ashtrays, a large serving vessel, numerous tankards, and a capacious cigar box, matched only be a salver of heroic proportions.

Oysters nowadays are so dear that the fortnightly stout-and-oyster suppers have become things of the past, and the breakfast parties held twice a term are oysterless. It is only now at the annual dinner that oysters are consumed – but in the noblest of surroundings, for the dinner is held, every Lent term, in the Prioress's Room, one of the oldest rooms in Jesus, part of the original nunnery on which the college was built.

One unwritten principle of the club is that it should consist of men from widely varying disciplines, both academic and otherwise. In 1969 its numbers included a historian, a theologian, an architect, a student, an economist, a lawyer, a veterinary surgeon and, to lend an air of ineffable respectability, the college chaplain. A glance through the minutes of past meetings shows that the club has seen a wide variety of personalities. Perhaps the most startling character was a certain Ewart Scott Grogan who came up in 1894, ostensibly to read law, but who soon transferred his interest from that rather dry subject to more enthralling pastimes. Two years after his arrival, he was summarily dismissed. The cause of his departure was a goat, loosed by Grogan in the rooms of a don who had gone away for the night. The goat evinced a fondness for the taste of paper and furniture stuffing, matched only by the Natives' delight in oysters. Unfortunately the don was not a dietitian, and showed no enthusiasm over this interesting repast.

One entry in the minutes records a club foray into a fellow undergraduate's rooms, which resulted in the almost total wreckage of that unfortunate's living quarters. But then in those days things were far more civilised . . . a bill for damages was submitted, approved, and subsequently paid by the culprits with the best of feeling.

Glancing through the pictorial record of members past and present, one is forcibly struck by styles of dress and appearance which have faded away – and in some cases returned. The caps, the wing collars, the hugely knotted ties! The moustache and single eyeglass! The centre partings and solemn faces! The Oxford bags turned up over the turn-ups! Exotic blazers the like of which are now seen only at Henley or in the King's Road. . . . The record stops in 1914, to take up again in 1920. And now for a few years the undergraduates look more like dons. An occasional smile appears in the late twenties, only to disappear in the thirties. Today, the facial expression is similar to that of ninety years ago – but how much more expensive the oysters!

P. M. HUBBARD

Ioan and the Tabriska

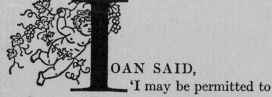OAN SAID,
'I may be permitted to
congratulate you, Excellency?' He wanted very badly to run a
finger round inside the collar of his nigh-necked tunic, but instead
he brought his heels together and sketched a bow, with his hands
politely at his sides. In any case, he meant what he said. The thing
had been a tremendous success, and he had had too much to do
with organising it not to feel the glow of placid excitement that
supervenes on a success of that sort.

The ambassador took his cue. His face did not soften, because it
had long since passed the point where it could, to any identifiable
extent. But he was pleased, and found himself unable to hide his
pleasure. It was not Ioan's congratulations he was pleased with.
Those were an expected formality. He was pleased with the success.
He said, 'Thank you, Ioan. Your own contribution has been considerable. It will not be forgotten. These things count, Ioan. It is
not, perhaps, the way we should choose of extending the Republic's
authority, but we have to remember whom we are dealing with.
One cannot hope to influence an alien and essentially hostile culture

by ignoring altogether its own shibboleths, even though we recognise them as decadent and effete.' He checked himself and pulled in his diaphragm sharply. Indigestion, thought Ioan. It was the esperons in the boranadi sauce. He had watched him, earlier in the evening, shovelling them in with only just the necessary regard for the effete shibboleths of an alien and essentially hostile culture. He had watched him with a mixture of satisfaction and concern, because the ambassador's digestion was a key factor in his own working conditions. But he thought the situation was in hand. His Excellency would be all right in the morning.

The ambassador, having for reasons of physical convenience drawn himself up to his full height, went on from a suitable mental elevation. 'The time will come, Ioan, when we shall speak to them with our own voice. We shall not need, then, to pretend to the values which our own ideologies reject. But for the present we play them at their own game and by their own rules, as we do at football.' He was pleased with the analogy, and went after it. 'The bourgeois plutocracies invent football for their own amusement. We do not reject it. We take it over, we intensify it, we give it a significance, limited but real, in our own culture. And we beat them at it.' He blinked for a moment as the result of the last international match came simultaneously into both their minds. But he was not going to let go of an interesting ideological gambit because of a minor deviation in fact. 'It counts, Ioan,' he said. 'It counts. It is the same with this evening. Our good friend Paralin represents the Republic in the kitchen just as the great Vieron represents it in goal. You did well to bring him. Is he' – the ambassador felt for the form of words he wanted, failed to find it, and said more or less what was in his mind – 'is he reconciled to the position?'

Ioan smiled, slightly and deprecatingly. He was suddenly aware that his feet were hurting him, and he wanted more than ever to loosen his collar. Everything required by the situation had been said on both sides. He wished the ambassador would go upstairs and take his own shoes off and start drafting his report. He said, 'Paralin is an artist, Excellency. An artist welcomes the widest possible audience. It is the same with our musicians. Or, as you so rightly say, our footballers. They enjoy, as artists, the applause of La Scala or of Wembley Stadium. But that does not mean that they would choose to live in Italy or England rather than in their own fatherland.' He knew as well as the ambassador that the slightest suspicion of such an unfortunate preference on the part of any of these artists would make their chance of performing before a wider

70

audience very small. But it was the ambassador's hare, and if the ambassador could let it jink round the occasional fact, so could he.

'Precisely,' said the ambassador. 'We all, in our way, serve. Vieron in his goal, Paralin in his kitchen, I in my embassy. And this evening the good Paralin's performance was superb.' He straightened up again as the superbness of the performance came home to him. He said, 'Please convey to him my appreciation.'

'I will, Excellency, I will.'

The ambassador nodded, turned and went up the wide stairs. As he went, one of his hands disappeared in front of him and busied itself with the buttons at his waist. Ioan, his finger in the collar of his tunic, watched him go. He ran his finger round to the back of his neck, first one side then the other. Then he sighed and went back along the hall.

Paralin was alone in the small room beyond the kitchens. He was eating, very delicately, a plate of cold white meat and a green salad. There was a glass of pale wine beside his plate, and in front of it a book propped up against the bottle. The book, like the bottle, was French. He nodded when Ioan came in, but his eyes went back to the book. He was a small man. His hair was grey and cut very short, and his skin, in that subterranean light, almost exactly the same colour as the wine. 'So?' he said.

There was no second chair, but Ioan sat on the unoccupied end of the table. He took one foot off the ground and revolved it cautiously round the ankle. Then he put it down again, regretfully, and lifted and revolved the other. He could not take both feet off the ground and remain facing Paralin. 'A triumph,' he said.

Paralin went on reading and eating. He seemed able to do both at once, but he had no eye to spare for Ioan. 'They liked it?' he said.

'They adored it.'

'Including the Frenchman?'

'Especially the Frenchman.'

Paralin nodded. He mopped his mouth, still very delicately, with a frayed but perfectly white linen napkin, and drank half his glass of wine. He lowered the glass, looked for a moment at the other half and drank that too. Then he mopped his mouth again. 'So,' he said.

'His Excellency,' said Ioan, 'asked me to convey to you personally his appreciation. A superb performance, he called it. He said that, like the great Vieron in his goal and himself in his embassy, you were serving the Republic.'

Paralin put his plate aside. Then he took the book away from the bottle and put that aside too. He put it face down on the table, open, so that his place was not lost. Then he raised his eyes and looked at Ioan. 'Vieron?' he said. 'His Excellency said that?'

Ioan nodded. Paralin took his eyes from Ioan and looked all round the white-tiled walls of the room. He looked at the single light hanging from the ceiling and at the single small window, uncurtained but heavily barred. He pushed his chair back from the table and took hold of the table edge. He lifted the two feet at his end a little off the floor, but without upsetting Ioan off the other end. Then he looked at Ioan again. His eyebrows went up, asking a question. Ioan shook his head. 'So,' said Paralin. 'That Vieron. Do you know him?'

'Of course.'

Paralin lifted the bottle, now free of the book, and poured himself another glass of wine. He did not offer any to Ioan. 'A baby,' he said.

'But a great performer,' said Ioan. 'And so a source of glory to the Republic.'

Paralin sipped his wine. 'When Vieron,' he said, 'projects himself across the goalmouth –' He put his glass down gently on the table and then, suddenly and unnervingly, lurched sideways, head back, throat muscles straining, fingers clutching at the gently spiced air of the kitchen. He looked less like a footballer than a photograph of a footballer taken with a long-distance lens and processed on newsprint. He did not get out of his chair. 'When he does that, this baby Vieron,' he said, 'he has in mind the glory of the Republic?'

Ioan had stopped swinging his leg while Paralin demonstrated, but otherwise he showed no sign of involvement. 'I think he is thinking of the ball,' he said. He began swinging his leg again, and Paralin, sitting straight in his chair, lifted his glass and drank.

'He is thinking of Vieron thinking of the ball,' he said. 'The ball, I grant you, but Vieron first. Vieron first, the ball next. The Republic – that I cannot say. I have never discussed the Republic with Vieron.'

Ioan said, 'But he serves.'

'He is paid,' said Paralin. 'And the people who pay him are pleased by what he does. Also, no doubt, they take credit for it. But he plays football to please himself.' He finished his wine, looked carefully at the bottle and put the cork back into it. The bottle was still half full. 'You, now,' he said, 'you serve. What you do you do for pay, for promotion, for power, for security – I do not know, perhaps even for the glory of the Republic. But not to please yourself. Do not tell me you please yourself by your work. You please His Excellency. This evening you have pleased His Excellency. But your feet hurt, your collar is too tight, you have indigestion or you are hungry, I do not know which. You want to go up to your room and take off that ridiculous fancy dress and be easy, but instead you come down here to tell me that, like Vieron and His Excellency, I have served for the glory of the Republic.' He put out a hand and took up his book. 'Which,' he said, 'I do not think you believe.'

'No?' said Ioan.

'No,' said Paralin. 'I serve, yes. I have served since I was a boy. I served the Avrilions. They were an effete and decadent aristocracy. They knew what food meant. Now I serve the Republic. I serve the Republic with torienas and sucking-pig and esperons in boranadi sauce, all in the same meal, like a shopkeeper putting all his goods in the window, in case the customers should think he has not got what they fancy. I think His Excellency has indigestion.'

'I think so too.'

Paralin shrugged. 'That is for you to worry about.'

'But you please yourself.'

Paralin put his book down on the table again. 'I?' he said. 'I please myself? I do not please myself. I create. I create beauty and perfection. That is never a pleasing thing to do. It may please others. I do not know, and it does not concern me. But I do not please myself, not like the great Vieron.' He began to move sideways in his chair, but Ioan got up quickly from the table.

'All right,' he said, 'all right. Not like Vieron. I understand.'

Paralin sat back in his chair and took up his book again, and Ioan went to the door. He went a little gingerly, but with dignity and determination. 'At least,' he said, 'we understand each other.'

Paralin said, 'God forbid,' and turned to his book, and Ioan went back upstairs.

He went up the narrow stairs between the white walls and through into the service rooms. Everything was quiet and in its place, with cloths draped over polished things on trays and a dim light burning. Even when he came out into the hall, the feeling of a place closed down for the night was very strong. The front door was shut and bolted, and outside, not too far away, a foreign policeman with time on his hands kept watch over this tired outcrop of the Republic, isolated in the middle of the huge, wide-awake city. The state rooms were empty, but the shut-in air smelt of food and cigar smoke. The lift-man was off duty. Ioan went quietly up the wide carpeted staircase. He unbuttoned the collar of his tunic as he went.

Even upstairs there was no one about. He went past the doors of the conference rooms and the library and His Excellency's suite, up the next flight of stairs, narrower and steeper now but still carpeted, to the offices and record-rooms and telephone-rooms of the second floor. Here life began again. The doors were shut, but there were lights and voices behind some of them. At the bottom of the wooden stairs he stopped and listened. The voices went on behind the doors, but no one came out. Ioan sat down on the bottom stair and took his shoes off. They smelt, not grossly but significantly, of warm leather and sweat. He picked them up and went on up the stairs. The wooden treads were cool and smooth under his socks, and his toes spread themselves gratefully. He did not bother about the third floor at all. He did not think he would meet anyone now, and if he did, it did not matter. He went quickly up the last flight and let himself into his room on the fourth floor. He put his shoes down inside the door but did not put on the light. There was enough light from the window, even at this height. He shut the door behind him and went across to the window and looked out.

He never seemed to get over the fascination of this. The window was open a little at the top, and the air that seeped in smelt of damp stonework and soot and, even up here, the faint exhalation of the thousands of cars that moved ceaselessly through the enormous maze of streets five floors down. The coping stones of the cornice stretched across the bottom of the window and on each side of it, not quite visible, the glistening slates sloped back to the gaggle of chimneys and ventilation shafts and wireless aerials that topped the roof. Beyond the cornice, in string upon string of parti-coloured lights, the city spread down to the invisible river and up to the hills beyond till they vanished in the luminous orange haze; and even that was not the end of the city.

The room behind him was very small. It had been a servant's room once, when the house was a private house and the city half its present size, and it was still a servant's room. Paralin was right. He did not enjoy his work, as Vieron did and as he thought the ambassador did when he had not got indigestion. He certainly knew nothing of Paralin's unconcerned dedication to perfection. He did not even work for the glory of the Republic, except incidentally. Except incidentally, none of them did. He served because he had come a long way in the service and meant to go further yet, even in shoes that hurt his feet. Meanwhile, what he smelt and saw from his window still made him giggle, because he could not properly believe that it was there or that he was where he was. It seemed too far from anything he recognised to be taken seriously, except for the purposes of his work.

He turned away from the window and switched on the light. He took off his tunic and hung it up in the wardrobe. He washed his face, neck and hands in the wash-basin, and took off the peculiar tight trousers that went with the tunic. He emerged, in singlet and pants, as undifferentiated Caucasian man. He was a slight, wiry man with bristling hair and the anxious face of the educated peasant. There was a fine steel chain round his neck and a key on the chain. It hung just inside his singlet, nestling among the black hairs on his chest. It was his badge of office. He was immensely proud of it, only no one was supposed to know it was there. He put on a shirt and tie over it, and then the blue suit with the built-out shoulders which he wore for going out. It did not occur to him that this was much more his national costume than the clothes he had just taken off. He thought it put him on terms with the city, where much of his work lay, even though he still did not believe in the city half as much as he believed in his work. Finally he put on a pair of square black shoes which went with the suit and did not hurt his feet. Then he was ready.

He put the light out and went back to the window. He pulled the top further down and sniffed the damp air which was so different from anything else he remembered. It was still exciting, but when you got down to ground level, it was never the same. There was very little real excitement in the city when you came to grips with it: it was only exciting from on top. He pulled the window up, checked what he had in his pockets and went out into the corridor. The door of his room clicked shut behind him. He walked quietly along the corridor and went down the stairs.

He let himself out by the little back door into the mews. It was this door he had the key of, hung on the steel chain round his neck. Only two other people in the embassy had the key of this door. He used it sometimes during the day when it did not seem appropriate, because of what he was going out for, to go down the front steps under the flag of the Republic and past the saluting policeman. He used it at night because it saved trouble and was less conspicuous. It was not so much a private door as a non-diplomatic one. All the other embassies in the city had similar doors and all the interested parties, of whom there were many, knew where they were and pretty well who used them. Somebody might even at this moment be sufficiently interested to note and record his quiet passage through the mews. If they were, it did not worry him. He was not on duty, not even on his way to one of those neither precisely arranged nor wholly fortuitous meetings on park benches or underground platforms with people he could get on with because they were as much out of place in the city as he was. He did not want to meet anyone. He did not even know exactly where he was going, but he knew what he was going out for. He was hungry.

He was a little ashamed of this. Paralin had seen he was hungry, but he had not admitted it. He would have liked to enjoy the kind of food the embassy had given its guests. It ought to be a virtue in him that he did not, but he did not find that this carried much conviction. What he would have liked would have been to enjoy the food as the ambassador enjoyed it, but with a better digestion, and then, like the ambassador, dismiss it as ideologically unsound. Not for the first time in Ioan's experience, the ambassador was getting the best of both worlds. On the other hand, he had now got indigestion, whereas Ioan was merely hungry. The ambassador might or might not be all right in the morning, but Ioan's hunger could be cured in a matter of minutes. All he had to do was decide what to eat and go to the appropriate place and eat it. He had not yet made his decision, but meanwhile he was walking in the general direction of food.

He knew what he really fancied. He fancied tabriskas fresh from the marsh-pools of the river valley where he had grown up. You ate them with cresses and curds and the leathery girdle cakes they went in for in those parts. They were not the sort of thing Paralin would have prepared for the Avrilions or would now, in his present manifestation, prepare for the French ambassador. They did not cost enough. But they were good food for a hungry man, and to Ioan they were a natural ingredient of his northern boyhood. Only no one in the city had heard of tabriskas, and in any case they did not travel. An hour out of the brackish water and they were finished. He came out of the mews into the brilliance of the street and found it, as always, too wide for comfort.

Nevertheless he went on, walking with the quick, rather padding step he had inherited from generations of men who used walking as the normal way of getting from place to place. He always walked when he could. It was only as a city that the city was fantastically big. On the ground the distances were nothing to a man who walked like that.

Twenty minutes' steady walking brought him to the part of the city where the restaurants were. The mere walking made him feel better. His feet no longer hurt, and the unsatisfactory oddments which, preoccupied and faintly resentful, he had picked out of the dinner had gone from his stomach. It was empty now, with the conscious and not uncomfortable void under the diaphragm that was one of the pleasures of life provided you had the means, not too far removed, of filling it. He still did not know what he was going to eat, but there was no hurry. All the restaurants would be open for a long time yet, and he would enjoy another quarter of an hour's anticipation.

The streets were narrower here and brilliantly lit. The pavements were crowded, and the cars slid endlessly between the moving walls of people. Ioan sauntered, consciously detached from it all but taking it all in. This was where the girl-shows were as well as the restaurants. They were all exactly alike. Each had little glass windows full of photographs of girls in determinedly suggestive poses and a hatchet-faced barker at the door under the ornamental lights. Shoddiness set in so close inside the door that it was visible from the pavement. Ioan had never been inside one of them, because it might set people talking and make difficulties in his work. Rightly or wrongly, he assumed that the moment he was inside the fact would be known. He enjoyed the photographs, but he did not really believe in them. They made him giggle, as the city made him giggle, by their sheer improbability, but he knew there was a catch in them somewhere. Sex was something quite different and much less complicated. The girls who worked at the embassy were hand-picked and had their duties at all hours. They were posted with sufficient regularity to obviate staleness, and Ioan, with his key round his neck, had a reasonable right of pre-emption. The girls, as a matter of course, saw the key, but as everybody in any case knew he had it, this did not matter, and it made them the more anxious to oblige. He looked at the photographs with a pleasantly detached curiosity, but the barkers never asked him to come inside. They were professionals, as he was, and were not going to waste their breath. Looking at the girls was only window-shopping. It was the restaurants he was really thinking of.

They were spaced at intervals along the street whichever way you walked, and all of them were special. None of them was simply a restaurant. There were vegetarian restaurants and fish restaurants and steak-houses, restaurants where they served the food as if it was a sacrament and restaurants which put all their money into the

floor-show and hoped you would not notice the food in the pre-
vailing excitement. There were some that were merely specially
expensive or specially cheap. But mainly they were national
restaurants. Already they represented a fair cross-section of the
United Nations, and every time he came this way there seemed to
be a new one. Western Europe and the Far East were long established in multiple representation, but the gap between the two was
being steadily filled in. It was the gap Ioan knew most about. Some
of the countries there ate such terrible food at home that he
wondered by what depths of prevarication the restaurateurs found
something to serve which the city could stomach even as a novelty.
But he was not in the mood for experiment. He was hungry.

He hesitated for a moment at a Hungarian restaurant, considering the possibility of *halaszlé* or *pörkölt*, but the photograph of
a girl in the next window distracted him. She was a big blonde girl,
staring into the camera with startled eyes and her legs so far apart
that only a casual hand stood between the proprietors and the
unavoidable intervention of the police. By the time he was past her
the *halaszlé* was forgotten. But he could not go on like this. Hunger
was beginning to undermine his judgment and resolution. If he did
not make up his mind soon, he would find himself eating American
chop suey behind a plastic bamboo curtain or tinned squid in front
of a coloured photograph of Mount Fujiyama. He still wanted
tabriskas, and the hungrier he got, the more plaintively he wanted
them. But he knew he was being unreasonable.

Austria offered him *faschierter schweinschlegel* served by blondes
in petticoats and ribbons, but he still moved on. It was the name
as much as the food that turned his stomach. *Schweinschlegel*, he
thought, what a language! If the ambassador meant what he said,
he did not see why the Republic should not open its own restaurant,
though the staffing would be an administrative nightmare. But
even then they would not have tabriskas. Torienas, no doubt, and
esperons in the proper sauce, but not tabriskas, except in some
horribly distorted form. He imagined dehydrated tabriskas revived
in brine before being served to credulous enthusiasts with tired
watercress bought in bundles in the city markets. The thought
made him sadder than ever, and two tears rolled suddenly down
his cheeks. He was an emotional man when off duty, and hunger
made him worse. Through his tears he stared at the photograph of
a svelte brunette with her back to the camera. She had bent forward
until the camera man had told her, perhaps rather sharply, that
she must not bend forward any further, and what with her trying

to hold the critical angle and smile at the camera over her shoulder, the photograph, even seen through his tears, was full of a sense of strain.

There was a voice behind him.

Bolun said, 'If you gave her a push forward, she'd have to turn her face away, but the rest would be all right.'

Ioan turned, wondering if his tears were visible. Bolun was a junior member of the staff, several grades lower than Ioan. Ioan, who carried all these things in his head, knew that Bolun had been off duty this evening. He did not hold with the freedom the juniors enjoyed in such ways, but the ambassador believed in it, and of course no one who was any sort of risk would be on the staff at all. He said, 'It is very curious, but I don't think I like it.'

He spoke a little severely. Bolun looked at him in the bright light from the window. He said, 'It's curious, all right.' The barker looked at the two of them, wondering what they were saying, but he did not suggest their coming in.

Ioan said, 'I'm hungry. Have you eaten?'

'Hungry? Don't let Paralin hear you. What was the trouble? Too busy to eat?'

'I think Paralin knows. I do not like that kind of food. We put it on because we are dealing with people who respect that kind of thing. We play them at their own game. But I do not enjoy it.' He had an idea that he sounded even less convincing than the ambassador, especially to Bolun. This was unfair, because he spoke more from the heart than the ambassador had. He really was hungry, and he did not want torienas and sucking-pig and esperons, he wanted tabriskas. The injustice of it overcame him, and he turned his back on Bolun and the window, blinking his wet eyelids in the less brilliant light of the street.

Bolun said, 'I have eaten, but not since early. I think I am hungry too.'

'So,' said Ioan. 'Let us eat.'

Bolun said, 'What?' and Ioan said, 'I do not know. I have been thinking, and I do not know,' and Bolun nodded sympathetically, and they both turned again and gazed sadly at the bending brunette.

Against his better judgment the barker took a chance. He said, 'You two gents like to see the show? It's just beginning.' Whatever time of day it was, he always told everybody that the show was just beginning.

Bolun spoke to him in the beautifully correct accent the Republic

80

insisted on in all its representatives abroad. He nodded towards the brunette and said, 'That one, tell me, is she in it?'

The barker looked at the photograph as if he was noticing it for the first time, as in fact he very likely was. 'Her?' he said. 'We've got three or four girls as good as her. If you gents would like –' but Bolun said, 'And tell me, does she go further in the show than in the photograph or further in the photograph than in the show? Further down, I mean,' he added. 'It is a legal matter, perhaps?' He was genuinely interested. Law was his special subject.

'Ah,' said the barker, 'you'd be surprised at the tricks some of them get up to. If you gents –' but Ioan said, 'I am hungry. I was thinking I should like tabriskas.' He spoke to Bolun in their own language. He even used the northern dialect. Bolun was a northerner too.

Bolun said, 'Ah, tabriskas!' and the barker said, 'Tabriskas, you said? That where you're from? Gawd, I remember tabriskas. In the war. Forty-four, it must have been, but I haven't forgotten. There was a girl called –' He stopped and shook his head. 'Can't remember her name,' he said, 'but I remember the tabriskas.' He stopped again, looking from one to the other of them. 'But I never seen them here,' he said.

Illustrations by Peter Morter

IVOR DRUMMOND

Death in the Priva

M ARISTIDE NERO'S
private dining-room was the best part
of the Hôtel de la Libération. And the rest was very good. To be
asked to the private room was an unusual honour. Great winegrowers sometimes dined there, foreigners seldom, amateurs never.

The hotel was an hotel – it was possible, though difficult, to
stay there – but primarily it was a place to go and eat.

The building was on the edge of a village in the Cevennes, forty
kilometres from Nîmes as the crow flies but an hour by road, even
in Sandro Ganzarello's car, and even though the car (to the terror
of his passengers) was driven by Sandro. The house had medieval
cellars, and had acquired over the centuries, like the ruins of Troy,
successive strata each identifiable by period. The tower had been
added in 1910 by a man from Lyon. It had been meant to turn a
big farmhouse into a small château; oddly enough it had succeeded.

After the war the property was acquired by M. Nero, who
sometimes said his family came from Menton. He brought with him
a *chef* from Bordeaux, a *sommelier* from Tain, large ideas, and all
the money in the world. The old great kitchen was turned into a
new great kitchen. Larders were filled with scrubbed pine shelves,

82

ining-room: a story

sculleries with aluminium, and the cellars with wine. (M. Nero somehow came, in 1949, by a large quantity of 1947 claret.) There were half-a-dozen bedrooms upstairs. The bedrooms were not important. American visitors would not have been impressed by them. M. Nero was not impressed by American visitors.

In fact M. Nero seemed not to be impressed by anything: not by Michelin, which nevertheless gave him two out of a possible three: not by the price of Charollais beef or partridges or duck or the almost unobtainable vintage cognac, or the terrifying post-war wages of his principal servants. Not by people who waded through his *menu gastronomique* nor by film-stars who wanted steak and chips. He had acquired fame; he knew he merited it; there were no signs that it impressed him. He had invested a lot of money; he was making a lot of money; there were no signs that he was much interested in that either. His ambition was limited, clear, and firmly stated. He wanted to own the best restaurant of its size in France. In Paris, in Geneva, in Milan, even in London and New York, there was a growing school of thought that said that he already did.

M. Nero's favourite clients were, naturally, Frenchmen. Fat Frenchmen. They approached the business of eating with almost professional, critical, clinical exactness. They discussed the menu with subdued passion. They ate course after copious course with devout greed. They said almost nothing until seven or eight successive, contrasted, subtly complementary *plats* had melted off the table, disappeared between damp lips, been solemnly masticated, and descended into the splendid barrels of their torsos. By these people, M. Nero knew, he must be judged. If they said he was the best, he was the best.

So there was no question of his being at any pains whatever to single out for honour American millionaire yachtsmen, or Italian millionaire counts, or aristocratic English débutantes. It was thought in the restaurant all the odder that a party of three – one each of these unimportant categories – should be entertained by M. Nero, that bright September day, in his private room for luncheon.

The private room was in the tower – the high square folly built by the man from Lyon to turn a modest fortune made from sausages into landed gentility. The walls were immensely thick, as though to protect the sausage-maker from the indignant ghosts of pigs. The windows were small, the battlements fanciful, the stairs narrow and dangerous. The room, when you reached it, was a marvellous embodiment of bourgeois French *goût sans goût* – a room devoid of design, of conscious decoration, of anyone's ever having said: '*That* would look nice *there*.' It was not meant to be looked at: it was meant to be eaten in. The walls were mustard yellow, the curtains khaki, the carpet indescribable. But a huge sideboard of hideous varnished oak bore the instruments required to celebrate the sacrament of eating: knives and tureens and chafing-dishes, glasses and decanters, pepper-mills and salt-mills, oil and various vinegars and home-made mysteries in small dark flasks.

A pale young waiter called Louis waited in the room. He was a find and a particular protégé of M. Nero. Some even said he was the *patron*'s natural son: but the *patron*'s single-minded passion for his restaurant seemed to most people to exclude the likelihood of lesser passions; it was generally agreed that M. Nero approved of the boy because he was a good waiter.

Louis waited, his napkin over his arm, for the jovial solemnities to begin. Feet tittupped on the stairs; the door opened; an astonishing blaze of gold burst into the room: the head of the English girl.

Louis was briefed. He knew about this girl. She was Milady Jennifer Norrington, daughter of an English earl, and although

84

she looked sixteen she was more. He had been told the girl was handsome; no one had warned him she was beautiful. She was beautiful. The simplicity of her dress, to a knowing French eye, concealed neither its expense nor the magnificence of the figure that it partly covered.

Louis bowed. The girl greeted him in casual, accurate French. She smiled briefly. The smile etched a dimple – a single dimple, in the left cheek only. Louis thought she was the most attractive girl he had ever seen. He was doubtless right. He sighed, because of the orders he had been given.

Louis bowed again, differently: because into the room came now, like a tiger with Latin blood, an enormous Italian. Louis's briefing said: il Conte Alessandro di Ganzarello. 'You will think he is ugly but women do not find him ugly.' Huge shoulders in a Savile Row suit, bright blue eyes in a dark face, under greying dark hair. A vivid and spectacular personality (thought Louis, but in a waiter's different words), a great steel spring under tight control.

'Do not despise,' Louis's briefing had continued, 'the American.' The warning was necessary because the third guest was not impressive. He shambled into the room as though the stairs had exhausted him. He was slim and middle-sized; he looked neither strong nor brave. Green eyes blinked apathetically from an unremarkable face; mousy hair had resisted the brush, and stuck out childishly from the back of his head. Louis had been told: 'Many people have been deceived. Do not be deceived.'

So Coleridge Tucker III, least explicable of M. Nero's honoured guests, stumbled into the room and said: 'Goddam exhausting, all those steps.'

The host came into the room last. Louis bowed a fourth time. His bow was brisk and businesslike; it had the quality of a salute – 'Platoon on parade, sir, and ready for your inspection.'

M. Nero looked the part. He was small and plump and dark. Button eyes peeped out, with cautious amiability, between puffy white lids. His chin was multiple, shiny, polished, blue. His hair was thinning, grey, brushed flat to a narrow skull. His short-legged body was clad in a black suit of local cut, his feet in black shoes of intricate design. His socks were purple and fitted tight to tiny ankles. One imagined chubby, polished white legs.

'Please sit here on my right, Lady Jennifer. M. le Comte on my left, please? And Mr Tucker, will you consent to occupy the bottom of the table opposite? Or if you wish,' M. Nero smiled – his smile was charming – 'consider it the top.'

M. Nero's English was excellent. He explained that he had learnt it before the war, when working for a company that exported olive oil, and had improved it as an agent for British Intelligence. 'A very small agent,' he said. 'My superiors saw that I was too fat and too frightened to be an important spy.'

Jenny sat down and grinned at M. Nero. You had to respect him as a professional, and you had to like him as a person. On every subject except food and drink he was modest and self-mocking, with that European humour of understatement that is falsely supposed to be a British speciality.

Louis gave each of them a narrow glass of chilled *blanc de blancs*. Not frozen, so that it anaesthetised like a dry martini or a julep, so that the flavour of the wine was hidden inside a glacial shock, but refreshingly cold.

Louis handed round menus. The menu was almost the only phenomenon at the Hôtel de la Libération that was deliberately ostentatious. Some of it was printed, some typed in muddy blue carbon, some handwritten. The names of the dishes were apt to be long. There were no prices on the four in use in the private room.

Jenny, opposite one of the little windows, saw the steep green slopes of the Cevennes under a blue and white sky. She heard cars arriving and distant voices that seemed to tremble with proper greed.

She sipped her champagne and turned to M. Nero and said: 'I feel like a baby let loose in a magic garden. Do you think you could possibly be absolutely sweet and make up my mind for me?'

M. Nero smiled at her. He saw a pink and gold and perfect face, wide blue eyes, lips parted over little white teeth, an expression of marvellous silliness. But he did not entertain guests in his private room for their beauty, nor did he entertain silly girls. He knew that this girl was clever and tough and sophisticated, and an expert on Bordeaux and on most of the wines of the Loire.

'I agree,' said Sandro Ganzarello in his deep sad voice. 'Choose for us, Aristide, so that we know we shall have the best *collazione* in Europe.'

M. Nero turned to him and again smiled. It was a smile of unexpected human warmth from a man who lived, as M. Nero lived, for a chilly artistic ideal. This Count, this rich *flâneur*, was well known everywhere from California to Kenya: well known at Lincoln Center, at Sotheby's, at Maxim's, at Chantilly, well known at the Hôtel de la Libération. A man whose life seemed supremely elegant and useless. M. Nero knew better.

'Goes for me too,' mumbled Colly Tucker. 'Goddam menu's as long as *Paradise Lost* and twice as heavy. And, frankly, Aristide, although my French is just about perfect, as you know, there's a few items here which I have to admit I just don't know what they mean.'

M. Nero smiled a third time across the well-furnished table at the young American. Even Louis smiled. Everybody smiled at Colly, and in their pity and contempt there was nearly always affection. He was said to be the laziest man in the United States. He suffered fools gladly because he was too idle and too good-natured to get up and go away. He was immensely rich. In him, inertia became something positive, a grand exaggeration so far beyond normal human capacity that it took on a quality which was almost heroic.

M. Nero, who knew about him, knew how the apathetic mask belied the quick brain and dangerous courage below.

Colly rolled his eyes helplessly and put the menu down. He raised his glass as though it, too, was as heavy as *Paradise Lost.* He grinned and said, 'C'mon, chum, you do the work.'

M. Nero laughed – a rare, shrill sound never heard in the kitchen or the restaurant. 'Okay, my friends. I will choose. I think it will be more interesting if we do not all four eat the same meal. I believe it will be amusing if I choose the lunch that exactly fits each one of us. Why should we four, who are all quite different, be identically suited by the same menu? Eh? You understand me? Yves St Laurent dresses different ladies in different styles. So I design a *déjeuner* for you all, and for myself also. So we shall each have' – in M. Nero's voice rang a certain arrogant certainty – 'the perfect luncheon for each of us alone. The very best.'

'Divine,' babbled Jenny, 'what a sweet thought. The only thing is, I'm going to yearn for all the things all the rest of you have, because whenever I have something different that's what always, always happens.'

'Not today, Lady Jennifer,' said M. Nero positively.

He looked at each of them in turn: at Jenny, whose hair shone like the dancing reflection of the sun in moving water and whose single dimple came and went in her cheek like a recurring eddy in a clear stream: at Sandro, whose heavy Latin face was punctuated so vividly by those brilliant blue eyes: at Colly, soft-voiced and unremarkable and terribly tired and living an even more dramatic lie than the other two.

He looked from the faces to his menu. He pursed his plump lips into a little round 'O' of open mouth, so that he looked as though he was about to whistle demurely to a small, old, docile poodle. He frowned. His eyes narrowed to slits. He nodded to himself, very slowly, a number of times.

It was almost funny, but it was not funny. M. Nero looked (you might have said he was consciously aware of looking) like Toscanini studying a score. The whole performance was absurdly pretentious: but the others waited quietly, not smiling, because they knew it was entirely sincere.

Finally M. Nero nodded decisively. (He was one of Napoleon's marshals approving a plan of battle.) He picked up the wine list. This, in tooled leather, was the size and gave the appearance of a considerable volume, possibly of epic verse or of hagiography.

He studied again. He blinked rapidly. He turned the pages with the speed and skill of a card-sharp manipulating a pack. His teeth clicked together and be began to murmur to Louis.

Presently Louis would leave the room for the first course. The three of them would be alone with M. Nero.

Louis would be away from the room from time to time after that, until he had cleared away the last plate and left them (presumably) with coffee and the remarkable vintage brandy.

Jenny thought: When will Sandro do it? When will he tell this nice little fatty that we know he murdered three people three months ago?

Three months before – early June: a most unfortunate affair at the Hôtel de la Libération. A party of three had come to dine with M. Nero in his private room. A Herr Feld, stocky and middle-aged, with a bulging neck, from Nierstein, assumed to be a grower or shipper of hock. A lady companion called Fräulein Carlotta, assumed to be a lady companion. And a big young Teuton whose name no one caught, a secretary or personal assistant or sales manager.

They spent a long time in the private room with M. Nero. They went at last to three of the hotel's barely adequate bedrooms – three rooms which connected and which shared a gurgling bathroom.

No one heard anything during the night, but the screams of the chambermaid in the morning nearly took the roof off the hotel.

The girl and the young man were in bed together, naked, in the end room, which was his. Both were dead from multiple stab-wounds. Both were perversely mutilated. The room was awash with blood.

Herr Feld was in the bathroom, in a full bath. The tap dripped still into the bath, and in the serpentine convolutions of the pipes the water coughed and thrummed. The bath was red. Herr Feld had cut his wrists in the bath.

The rooms were locked. One glance told all. The police nodded wisely and agreed that nothing was to be gained by publicity.

'Karl Feldmann has been murdered,' said Sandro two days later, in Jenny's London flat, to Jenny and Colly.

'What it says, Fatty,' said Jenny, 'is suicide after a *crime passionnel*.'

'Goddam convenient,' said Colly. 'Saves us a lot of trouble.'

'Never in one million years,' said Sandro, 'would Feldmann commit suicide. *Mai*. But a professional blackmailer on such a big scale is likely to be much disliked, yes?'

'Yes,' said Colly. 'Me, I always thought blackmail could be defensible grounds for murder. Whoever did this is a public benefactor.'

'So this,' said Jenny, 'is one job we don't have to finish. What bliss. Let's go to the *Pays Basque* and do some trout fishing.'

'Carina, this is one job we do have to finish. Only now it is a new job.'

Within two days they knew M. Aristide Nero's history and reputation, and all that there was to be known about the Hôtel de la Libération. Within four days Sandro had unearthed, from among French friends of the racecourse and the covert and the auction-rooms, people who were customers of M. Nero and were known to him. Within six days they were lunching, under excellent auspices, in the restaurant of M. Nero.

They went again, then a third time. They began to rank as *habitués de la maison*. They got to know and like M. Nero, and to understand what had happened when his upstairs floors were puddled with blood.

'He is a man without a history,' said Sandro. '*Sempre, sempre*, that means a secret history, a shame, something to be hidden.'

'British Intelligence,' said Colly. 'We checked up, chum. He's levelling.'

'But before. The *società* of the oil. It was destroyed, the buildings, all the records. Did he work there? No one can know. *Where did his money come from?*'

'The poor little sweet pinched it during the war,' said Jenny, 'and Feldmann found out and blackmailed him.'

'*Certo.*'

'So Nero murdered him and the other two.'

'I think.'

'Oh dear.'

'Yes, I am sorry.'

'I don't see,' said Colly, 'that it's a thing we can possibly prove,

Sandro. The cops closed the case.'

'We cannot prove. The waiter Louis sees Aristide go to his own bed. The maid's key was downstairs with the other keys and had fingerprints of Feldmann and his whore and the maid. It could *not* be as it seemed to be, but we only know this because we knew Feldmann.'

'Feldmann,' said Jenny, 'was perfectly capable of a nasty murder.'

'Yes. The mutilation no. That was unnecessary trouble with no profit to follow. And the suicide after – *mille volte no.*'

'So what do we do?' said Colly. 'Let Aristide get away with it?'

'I don't know. I would like.'

'Me too,' said Jenny.

'I think we will talk to him quietly. It must be private. I will fix.'

'So?' said Jenny.

'Aha,' said M. Nero. 'So. I have painted three portraits and a self-portrait. With flavours, textures, perfumes, colours – with food and with wine.'

'Tell.'

'Oh no. *Du vin, Louis, vite, s'il te plaît.* You shall see. You shall trust me and it shall come as it comes. And after we will discuss. Have I painted the truth, like Leonardo and Holbein and Toulouse-Lautrec, or have I painted a surface, a lie, a flatterment, like Fragonard, like Ingres, like David?'

A gastronomic portrait. A person – four persons – painted in the pigments of *haute cuisine*.

Sandro thought: *Interessante ma un po scherzo.*

Colly thought: You could hang the ultimate result in the Guggenheim and no questions asked.

Jenny thought: If I'm *compôte de pêches et de fraises en Kirsch* I shall scream.

Louis went out softly.

Jenny and Colly both glanced involuntarily at Sandro: but he sipped his wine and asked about the truffle harvest.

Louis came back, with a laden tray and various bottles.

To Jenny he gave one dish, to Colly a second, to Sandro a third, and to M. Nero a bowl of soup. He opened the bottles and filled a glass from each.

The three looked at M. Nero. Only the hint of Jenny's dimple rippled the smooth pink-gold surface of her cheek.

Aristide Nero spoke: 'My friends, we begin to sketch the por-

91

traits. Lady Jennifer has *blancs d'œufs surprise*. Please eat. I do not want my *chef de cuisine* to become distressed by food growing cold which should be hot. I shall speak through my soup. You will pardon me. Now – Lady Jennifer must of course be a surprise. The dish must be unexpected, not as it seems. This is the first and most obvious; everything follows. What must the first impression be? Naturally an impression of purity, of innocence, of youth. The white of the eggs, you see, with a very little cream. And below? Ah, Lady Jennifer, you have already excavated a little with your spoon. Below the white, the yellow of the egg. The yolk. Not quite a surprise, but hidden, yes? Beneath the insipid exterior of *jeune fille* there is already a woman, a heart, the possibility of passion, of conception – please forgive me if I am rude. No? *Bien*. But beneath this warm and complete woman who is herself hidden from the world, there is something else. The big surprise. A strong mixture. Do you like it? It is not to the taste of everybody. *Foies de volailles*. Hare. Mushrooms. *Jus de viande*. Pepper. Cognac. Other things. It is strong and savoury, it is surprising. Am I painting the personality? The truth, not the surface? Below the pale innocence a passionate woman; below the woman a complex and dangerous *mélange* of animals and of the insides of animals and of strong drink.'

Jenny ate delicately, tasting the contrast between the bland egg and the powerful, subtle mixture below. She could not fail to recognise the justice of Aristide Nero's portrait. What was disturbing was that he knew. Nobody knew. How did he know? Why did he know?

Her wine was surprising in this place – a Herrgottströpfchen only two years old.

M. Nero said: 'I try to find you a companion to the *œufs surprise* which is very young, so? It must be, because you are. And very palatable, immediately pleasant, because you are. But it must not be a little wine to be drunk young, a little girl of a wine without character. Oh no. It must be a big wine with a hint of great character and hardness, with acid and a taste of stone.'

Jenny tasted the cold pale wine. Acid, hardness, stone. Whom has he been talking to?

In front of Sandro was a small bowl of a smooth, darkish, viscous mixture covered with little squares of fried bread. Sandro tasted it. It was new to him. It was delicious. He looked at Aristide Nero with raised eyebrows, a half-smile etching deep lines in his dark cheeks.

'*Tapenade Provençale*,' said M. Nero. 'A dark dish, that is obvious. (You forgive a direct reference to your complexion? Good.) And you must be painted in something naturally of the South. It must be strong, and taste of herbs and hard bright sunlight. But it must not be entirely of the Mediterranean. That would be the surface only. It must have something about it of England, traditional, like your clothes and all your guns and your dogs. So you have there black olives from Provence, dark and ripe, matured in that fierce sun. Yes? You see yourself in those olives? They have been put into a mortar with anchovies. That is part of what you taste. What else? Thyme, garlic, cognac, oil. All that you can taste. What else. Aha. *Moutarde anglaise*. There is the secret. So the portrait shows us – a mixture of Italian aristo, Sardinian bandit, and the interesting Mr James Bond.'

Sandro's face showed nothing except polite appreciation. He thought: While we have been examining Aristide, Aristide has been examining us.

His wine was a pale, hard, gold. He sniffed and tasted. It was sherry.

'Manzanilla, the driest in Jerez,' said M. Nero. 'The olives and anchovies and above all the mustard require a fortified aperitif. A simple wine would die, and it is not the wine that must die today. And for you the drink must be expensive, traditional, and international. *Voilà*.'

Voilà, thought Sandro. Louis stood like a statue. M. Nero drank his soup.

'For you, dear Mr Tucker,' said Aristide Nero, pointing across the table with his spoon, 'something clearly which seems simple and easy, something uncomplicated, a lazy dish. You have *Jambon Chablis*. No, not the wine. The dish has been created by a famous restaurateur in the town of Chablis, at the Hôtel de l'Etoile. Shallots and *extrait de viande* and a little vinegar make a *paté*, and it is gently heated until it is very, very hot. And then there is cream. But the cream must not boil. It is difficult. You must take very great care. That which appears simple is not simple, and that which appears lazy is not at all lazy. Properly, the ham should be peach-fed Virginia ham, but this is *jambon de Paris*. The painting is, I think, the same.'

The wine was a Pouilly Blanc Fumé of 1962.

'You taste the flint?' said M. Nero. 'Oh yes. Under the soft flavour of the grape the taste of flint, hard as iron. Oh yes.'

Colly thought: Jesus. What next?

'I myself,' said M. Nero, 'have, as you see, onion soup. It is dark, it is quite rich. The ingredients are humble. It is easy to make. There is nothing about it aristocratic, nothing at all. It is *cuisine bourgeoise*. It is even *paysanne*. It is what it is. It is not like any other dish. It is – shall I say? – sure of itself.'

Sandro raised his great head from the oily, savoury, superb mixture on his plate. 'You paint strange portraits, Aristide. Your pictures would not be recognised by our friends.'

M. Nero had finished his soup. He put down his spoon and sighed. The ghost of a belch announced a judgment of the soup.

He said: 'A Mr Feldmann, also Herr Feld, with also many other names, came here three months ago. He was going to destroy me. I was rich at the end of the war. How? Nobody in the world knows. Those who knew were dead. But Mr Feldmann knew. He died. Soon after, three strangers came here. They came again and again. They ask a few questions which were not the questions of people who come here to eat. In the war I learned to detect questions, to sniff them with my nose. These people ask questions not only here but in London and in Marseilles and Paris. Questions of Naval Intelligence, questions of the *Sûreté*. So I ask questions too. In the war I became expert at asking questions so that nobody knew any questions were being asked. I learned more, much more, than the world knows about the big Italian count and the pretty English child and the so-lazy American. I do not learn everything, as you have not learned everything. But I learned enough, as you have learned enough. You have finished the *hors d'œuvre*? They were nice? They were pure and safe, quite okay. Look at Louis.'

Sandro, Jenny, and Colly looked at Louis. He was standing by the door. He held a small automatic with a silencer. His face was still expressionless. He pointed the muzzle slowly from one to another.

'Louis is a very good shot,' said M. Nero. 'That is why he is here. He will shoot two of you certainly and perhaps three if you make rapid movements which he dislikes. His instructions in the event of trouble are to shoot but not to kill.'

'Good,' said Jenny unexpectedly.

'I do not want you killed by a fat bullet. I like you. And it would be inartistic. I did not mind how Feldmann died but I would prefer you to die elegantly. To my permanent grief I am not myself a creative artist in the kitchen – an impresario merely – but I understand and love the kitchen and I can manipulate it. So I kill you all three in my own way. Louis is not to kill you but to prevent

your escape. which he will assuredly do. Another pop will be the
pop, simply, of another bottle of champagne.'

Sandro said: 'Aristide, we came not to kill you or to denounce,
but to talk. We know that you had cause to kill Feldmann. We do
not disapprove of his death. He is better dead. The bodyguard
perhaps also, the girl perhaps not. It is a thing to discuss. There is
no need to kill us.'

'There is a very great need, M. le Comte. I killed many times to
become in a position to start the Hôtel de la Libération. I have
killed three times to protect it. I must *of course* kill three more times
to protect my hotel and my reputation and my life, which to me is
much more important than yours.'

'How are you going about it, chum?' asked Colly without anima-
tion or apparent interest.

'It is an idea which in other circumstances you might find
amusing. You each eat seven courses. Everything is different, yes?

I am still painting my pictures. There are different wines. Many of the courses will consist of two or five or a dozen different things. For each of you something, some one thing, will be poisoned. You will not have time to taste the poison. It is very powerful and quick. It is not, I fear, painless. Will it be in your *pointes d'asperges*, Lady Jennifer? Your *vin de Bourgogne*, Count? Your Camembert, Mr Tucker? The *pommes Parisiennes*? Which individual one of the *pommes Parisiennes*? You must eat all, you see, because my *chef de cuisine* has given you just exactly the right quantities and I cannot permit that he is offended. If you will not eat Louis will shoot you in the thigh or the shoulder, or the hand, or the ear. You will not then enjoy eating but you will still eat, because there are many fat cruel bullets in that pistol.'

A silence followed this speech, which was an exceptionally long one for M. Nero to make on any subject except food.

Someone knocked on the door. Another waiter came in with the second course. He was older than Louis, thicker, equally pale. He glanced incuriously at the gun and at the three guests of M. Nero. There were plates on his tray under silver covers, and some wines. He began to serve the second course.

Jenny was given a *soufflé d'homard* with Puligny Montrachet.

'The texture and the delightful colour, it is you, yes? And that lobster had once big powerful claws. No longer. It is dead and its claws are dead empty shells. You no longer have claws, Lady Jennifer. You see I have painted the present and the future as well as the past.'

Jenny hesitated before affronting the perfection of the soufflé with her fork, before tasting the cold white burgundy. Louis's gun-muzzle swung lazily towards her. She thought: It's the whole thing or nothing. It can't be one bit of a soufflé. It's early in the meal. Here we go.

She lived.

Sandro speared each one of his *écrevisses à la Madame de Montespan* with distaste. Any one of them . . . the big cylindrical silencer wobbled towards his thigh. He ate them. He drank his Muscadet.

M. Nero beamed at him. Till the third course at least he lived.

Colly had a *sole à la Tête de Cervelle*, a variant of *sole Walewska* named after the auberge near Quimper where it was invented. Perhaps the scarlet slices of lobster-meat were Jenny's claws. Perhaps one of them carried the poison. Perhaps not. Louis's gun drifted. Colly tried to enjoy the subtlety of the sauce, and the dry assertiveness of the Chateauneuf du Pape blanc which accompanied his fish. He failed.

M. Nero ate a plain grilled trout. He explained that it was wild, and that when it was hooked it struggled. His pudgy white cheeks bulged and crumpled as he smiled at his guests. He drank a young Alsatian from Ste Odile.

The older waiter came and went. The next dishes were more elaborate.

Jenny's was a quail *en croute* with a sauce of some complexity.

'An English joke,' said M. Nero. 'It is a little bird. You see?'

Sandro had *faisan Montélimar*, which had nothing to do with nougat but plenty with artichoke hearts and Armagnac cuddling aromatic slices of breast-meat.

'I was partly guided,' said M. Nero, 'by the so misleading name.'

Colly was given *caneton à la belle Arlésienne*, made like a chicken Kiev but with something from Parnassus instead of butter inside.

'Nothing is more amiable and foolish than a duck,' said M. Nero. 'Prick this one with your fork, and *pouf!* you get a shock.'

'You prick me with your fork, Aristide,' said Colly. '*Pouf* to you, chum. My appetite's gone.'

'Louis?'

'Ah, let your boy shoot all he wants. I had bullets in my leg before.'

The gun was pointing at Colly.

Colly picked up his fork and waved it. 'Okay, okay, but I'm gonna have indigestion as well as be dead –'

The wagging fork distracted Louis momentarily, fractionally. Sandro's movement was so quick that it took even Jenny completely by surprise. The *faisan Montélimar* rose from the table and crashed juicily full into Louis's face. Louis fired – a pop like a champagne-cork from the silenced gun. The bullet crashed into Jenny's pastry and ricocheted from the devastation of her quail into the wooden edge of the window. Sandro rose and hit Louis on the neck with the heel of his hand. At the same moment Colly brought a chair down on the waiter's head. The gun fell. Jenny picked it up and pointed it sadly at Aristide Nero.

Louis was knocked out, lying like a doll in the corner of wall and sideboard. There was a trickle of blood over his left eye. His pulse was regular. His face was a mask of expensive gravy.

M. Nero sat expressionless.

'You were to eat presently,' he said to Sandro, 'the magnificent steak of an animal which was killed in the bullring at Arles. The bull killed a man before it died. I painted well, I think. What will you do, M. le Comte?'

Sandro was silent.

'Well, Sandro?' asked Jenny. The gun was heavy but she held it steady.

'What's the scenario?' asked Colly. He dropped the pieces of his broken chair and sank with a sigh into Jenny's.

M. Nero leaned forward. 'You permit?' He took Jenny's wine, the Haut Brion he had picked to go with her quail.

'Drink up,' said Jenny.

M. Nero drank deep. He swigged (to Jenny's surprise) a claret which merited sipping. A change came over his face. His pink lips stretched back from his teeth (excellent imitations) and the pupils of his eyes swivelled and disappeared under his upper lids. He shuddered as though hit by a bolt of electricity and gave one short, high, gargling, horrible cry. He fell back into the chair and the glass dropped and shattered.

'My wine,' said Jenny. 'Gracious.'

Colly that evening said: 'You know what I think? The guy who killed Feldmann deserved a medal, not death by poisoning.'

Sandro said: 'One death is never enough. It is not a thing that can be permitted. And it was not a nice murder. The unfortunate whore, and mutilated also. And his design for killing us – there was a cat and a mouse, yes? Three blind mice. It was a little sadistic.'

'What I can't forgive,' said Jenny, 'is the *soufflé d'homard*. Texture, indeed! And fancy putting poison in Château Haut Brion.'

'*Lèse majesté?*'

'Criminal waste.'

Illustrations by Brian Pearson

Which is the World

DURING THE TEN YEARS
that we have been travelling the
world, fork in hand, we have come to know a mere three thousand,
four hundred and ninety-two restaurants. The gaps in our knowledge are immense.

For the present, we have lost our taste for the Soviet Union, and
we have not yet been able to swallow the China of Monsieur Mao
Tse-tung. But one question pursues us constantly: 'You know
restaurants more or less everywhere. What, then, is the best
restaurant in the world?'

Now the editor has asked us the same impossible question, and
we are going to try, without too many illusions of success, to
answer it. It is not a simple question. Moreover, there are two of
us, and naturally we do not always agree. This sort of debate runs
the risk of ending in bloodshed.

Also, we cannot do anything to change the fact that we are
French, and obviously tempted to think that our cuisine, as it is
prepared in France, is the best in the world. So we risk being
accused of chauvinism. *Tant pis.* Here, faithfully transcribed, is
our debate.

Christian Millau: The world's best restaurant . . . Yes, I've been
there but unfortunately I don't remember the name. It was on
25 August 1944. I was fifteen years old and the Allies had just

-reatest Restaurant?

❁ ❁ ❁

liberated Paris. I found myself perched on a Sherman tank. Around noon we stopped on a grassy strip along the Avenue Foch, near the Arc de Triomphe. The soldiers invited me to share their lunch. They gave me a box of K rations, a cup of Nescafé and a Camel. After four years of swedes, there I was in a fabulous new world, the epitome of refinement and opulence. The world's greatest restaurant? For me, at that point, it was an anonymous muddy tank. And even today, when I'm famished the restaurant that puts a fried egg in front of me is the best in the world.

Henri Gault: Yes, of course, food is like love – completely subjective and relative. But as we have to play the game, let's define our criteria. What is a good restaurant?

CM: A place where you can get a good meal. And the best restaurant is the place where you can get the best meal. This may sound simplistic, but it's the whole problem in a nutshell.

HG: People are often more influenced by the décor, the way the proprietor looks, or by their own mood than by whether the actual food is good or indifferent.

CM: We shall consider only the cuisine, or at least we shall try to keep from being swayed by anything else. Décor and atmosphere shouldn't count. But how shall we judge the quality of the cuisine?

HG: Escoffier said that talent consists of letting foods retain their natural flavours.

CM: Yes, any needless complication is unpardonable. Something obvious is necessarily something bad. The secret of genius in

cuisine, just as in fashion or music, consists of possessing it in the first place, and then of not allowing it to show too much.

HG: We can try a quick tour of the world, picking out the most representative restaurants.

First, the more underprivileged areas, gastronomically speaking: Eastern Europe, the Middle East – except perhaps for Lebanon, where the food is quite good – and Latin America.

CM: Those areas are out of the running. So are all those restaurants that serve what the English call 'international cuisine', which is nothing more than a pretentious collection of pseudo-French recipes.

HG: But we can't eliminate all the Anglo-Saxon countries without some discussion. There are some good, even great, restaurants in London, Montreal, New York.

CM: Of course. But all the good restaurants there have French or at least Italian chefs. The 'native' cuisine of the Anglo-Saxon countries will never take any honours.

HG: Let's eliminate all Africa. Except perhaps for Dakar.

CM: And particularly except for the *Maison Arabe* in Marrakesh, which I consider one of the world's top restaurants.

HG: Aren't you going overboard a bit?

CM: I'm going to explain why the *Maison Arabe* is so amazing. At the end of the last war, the Pasha of Marrakesh, Le Glaoui, met the

daughter of a Parisian restaurateur, Mme Sébillon, who had just moved to Morocco. One day he said to her: 'Except for my palace, there are no good restaurants in Marrakesh. Why don't you open one? I'll help you.' Le Glaoui had around 150 women in his harem. The main job of his wives, since he preferred young Parisian actresses for his personal diversion, was to do the cooking. Ten at a time they spent a week in the kitchens working under the direction of some formidable, all-powerful cooks. If a dish was spoiled, the guilty party was thrashed. Le Glaoui gave Mme Sébillon one of these fierce cooks to start her restaurant.

In no time the *Maison Arabe* became extraordinarily popular. The cook behaved like a queen. The proprietress was not allowed to see the food in the kitchen and the cook even refused to give her any of the recipes. Mme Sébillon worried: the cook was old. What would become of the restaurant when she died? After a time, the cook made a pilgrimage to Mecca. She returned penniless. When she asked Mme Sébillon for money, however, she was told: 'All right, but give me your recipes.' With this began an extraordinary deal: recipe by recipe, the old cook sold the secrets of some twenty great Moroccan dishes. Then she died.

And I can assure you that if you had tasted the chicken in lemon sauce, the pastilla, the stuffed fish, the magnificent salads served on large copper platters, you would agree with me.

HG: Perhaps. But let's continue eliminating.

CM: While we're on Eastern cuisine, you can forget about Greece, for the *Taverna Ta Nissia* in the Athens Hilton has come down a lot.

HG: Yes, but *Kanakis Garden* just outside Athens is still good.

CM: While we're at it, let's wipe the unfortunate State of Israel off the gastronomic map of the world for ever.

HG: With one reservation: the goulash at Fink's Rothschild Bar in Jerusalem.

CM: So let's move on to more likely places. The Far East, for example. You've been there recently. Go back over your route.

HG: A great variety of curries, the extraordinary, aromatic mulligatawny soup of Colombo, the satays of Malaysia (pieces of meat or meat patties, charcoal grilled), the *rijsttafel* of Indonesia. In a Balinese village square, surrounded by temples, I ate an admirable roast sucking pig.

In Macao, in the elegant restaurant of the *Estoril* casino-hotel, the Portuguese chef (who had never been to Portugal) prepared strange semi-Portuguese, semi-Indian dishes that were excellent, especially spiced chicken from Mozambique that was very hot but remarkable nevertheless.

The great Far Eastern cuisine is the Chinese. In France and England you get only a vague idea of what it is like. As far as I'm concerned, I feel I discovered true Chinese cooking in San Francisco, two years ago. There are 62,000 Chinese living there and they would not stand for substitutes. And even after visiting the main Chinese restaurants in Singapore and Hong Kong, I would choose San Francisco's *Imperial Palace* to represent Chinese cuisine. I shall never forget their Cantonese lobster, the pork fried in palm oil with green peppers, the dish of three eggs, the melon soup.

To my mind, Chinese cuisine is as subtle as the French – if not more so – as delicate, as flavourful, as varied. However, in both Hong Kong and Singapore the concept of a 'very good restaurant' simply does not exist. There are good dishes – among the best in the world – but they are never found together under the same roof. For example, to eat roast goose in Hong Kong – and it is exquisite with its browned skin steeped in soy sauce and honey – you have to go to a little restaurant, the *Yung Kee*, where you share your round table with pretty secretaries.

Those little *hors d'œuvre* they serve with tea from 8 to 11 a.m. are best at *Tai Tung*, the Peking duck at the *Princess Gardens* and at the *Peking*, the crab in black bean sauce at the *Paris Noodle*, the fabulous Yunan ham, which makes the best Parma ham seem like cardboard, at the *Siamese Birds-nest*, the 'beggar's chicken' cooked in clay at *Tin Hing Lou*. However, apart from these and a few other specialities that are cooked to perfection, the food in these restaurants as a whole would not put them in the 'great restaurant' category.

CM: I noticed the same thing in Formosa.

HG: In Singapore I did find a restaurant where everything seemed above average: the *Peking*. But to eat the best possible Chinese food there, you must order your meal in advance. Then everything becomes miraculously good.

CM: That proviso means eliminating Chinese restaurants entirely. Except perhaps for the one in San Francisco.

As far as I'm concerned, the same would apply to Oceania. In Tahiti I ate the best shrimps in the world and an extraordinarily delicate fish called mahimahi, but neither Tahiti, nor Samoa, nor certainly Hawaii, had a restaurant worthy of being chosen.

ʒ ❀ ❀ ❀ ❀ ❀ ❀ ❀ ❀ ɛ

HG: At this point there are just two restaurants on our list: your *Maison Arabe* and my *Imperial Palace*. Before we go on to Europe, let's see if we can add anything from North America. We have to be careful about our chauvinism, but at the same time we can't allow ourselves to flatter our American friends too much by over-estimating the virtues of their gastronomy.

CM: Which is always French. Because the Americans have an inferiority complex about food and as far as I know there isn't a single American restaurant that has built a top reputation on baked oyster pies, snapper soup, ham steak, not even on fried chicken, shad roe, soft-shell crab, clam chowder or other authentically American dishes. And it's really a shame. The Canadians have equally little self-esteem and also swear by French cuisine. None the less, these are my favourite restaurants: *Bardet* in Montreal and *La Saulaie* in Boucherville, near Montreal, *La Crémaillère* in Banksville, near New York, and the *Caribbean Room* of the Pontchartrain Hotel in New Orleans.

HG: Allow me to add *La Grenouille* in New York.

CM: Yes, I agree. And you will note that except for the Pont-chartrain, all these restaurants have French chefs. Anyway, that gives us some new restaurants to choose for our list.

105

HG: Let's come back to them later. First, let's go on to Europe. In England: nothing. *Mirabelle*, the *Grill Room* of the *Savoy*, the best French-style restaurants are good, but they would pass almost unnoticed in Paris, even in Brussels. As far as the English-style restaurants go, I prefer the *Guinea Grill* and *Baron of Beef*, excellent bistros with exceptionally good food but prepared without spark. I know you prefer the *Hunting Lodge*, but I've had some rather poor meals there. Finally, the excellent *Prunier* is not quite up to the level of the two Parisian Pruniers, which would never be ranked among the top five French restaurants. And the English countryside is horrible, except for a few old inns, like the *Mitre* at Hampton Court. To my mind Great Britain has nothing exceptional to offer to the gourmet.

CM: Nor does Ireland. Although the food is good at the *Russell* and particularly at the *Hibernian Hotel*. Scandinavia is more interesting, and at least three places deserve to be put on our list. First Copenhagen's *Coq d'Or*. I don't have as high an opinion of it as Temple Fielding, who considers it the best restaurant in the world: '*out of this world*', he said! But we must admit that the 'special Danish lunch' is amusing and reasonable. Danish food is always of good quality, nicely prepared and children like it very much. But obviously this is not great cuisine. The Swedes, who generally do not have good food, have one excellent restaurant, the gigantic and lighthearted *Operakällaren* where the Swiss chef – a guarantee of goodwill – prepares an exceptional turbot. But to my mind, the best Scandinavian restaurant is in Norway: *Dronningen*, near Oslo. Once you taste the raw salmon marinated in dill and served with boiled eggs, or the *poule de neige* (ptarmigan) with bilberries and cream, you will never dismiss Scandinavian chefs completely.

HG: I didn't say anything. I'm not attacking you.

CM: No, but I can see that you're about to. You will have us cosily back in France, in Paris and Lyon, after cheerfully eliminating the whole world.

} ❁ ❁ ❁ ❁ ❁ ❁ ❁ ❁ {

HG: We shall see. By the way, that marvellous restaurant in Oslo is, if I am not mistaken, closed all the year round.

CM: Not exactly: it closes from September to May. Let's go south. Germany. Since Berlin's *Horcher* moved to Madrid, I see only *Erbprinz* in Ettlingen, for its game from the Black Forest and its crayfish, and, at a pinch, *Walterspiel* in Munich, but that is open to debate.

HG: If you really look, you'll also find *Kottler's* in Berlin, *Peter Lembcke* in Hamburg, *Weinhaus Wolff* in Cologne, and others. Do you think we should put them on the list?

CM: No. Let's go to Holland. The only interesting restaurant I know there is the *Bali* in Amsterdam.

HG: Yes, but between us, the *rijsttafel* is better in Indonesia.

CM: As well as the *Coq d'Or* in Rotterdam, good but pretentious, and the *Dikker en Thijs* in Amsterdam, which is charming.

HG: For me, Dutch cuisine is a curse. A sort of German gastronomy, English style: heaviness leavened with boredom. Having said that, I must admit that the *Prinses Juliana* in Valkenburg is more than respectable. Marvellous fresh lobster (they have built their own lobster bed, for it is not near the sea), a beautiful saddle of lamb, smoked Dutch salmon, game and magnificent wines. This is a restaurant we can put in the second divison of our finals.

CM: That makes me think of how funny it would be to organise a tournament of gourmets and the winners could be our referees. Meanwhile, let's move on to the part of Europe where, next to France, the food is the best: Belgium. They have as many good restaurants there as we do. The *Carlton* and the *Villa Lorraine* in Brussels and *La Vallée* in Lorcé in the Ardennes rival our best. Especially *La Vallée*, which does not have the inconvenience of being located in a large city where it is hard to obtain good provisions, and where the clientele often imposes bad habits.

At the Carlton in the springtime, on tables decorated with flowers from the garden, what a pleasure to eat that vegetable unknown outside of Belgium, *'jets de houblon'*. And that other Belgian speciality with the nettles – the eel in green sauce – there is the best in the world.

As for the *Villa Lorraine* on the edge of the beautiful Soignes forest, generally everything is perfect, particularly the duckling with onions, but I have also had some pretty bad meals there. It's disgraceful, in a place like that, to serve that Belgian calamity, fried potatoes, at every turn.

At *La Vallée* in Lorcé, which looks like a charming hunting lodge,

107

the Ardennes ham, the trout, and the wild boar *tutti frutti* are simplicity itself and the greatest success.

HG: Simplicity at £8 or £9 a head, don't forget. I don't want to defend Spanish and Portuguese food, which is ordinary and heavy, but in Spain and Portugal, at least, simplicity is cheap. I don't mean the great restaurants with French cuisine such as the *Jockey* and *Las Lanzas* in Madrid, *Reno* in Barcelona, *Aviz* in Lisbon; or tending toward the German such as the remarkable *Horcher* in Madrid – which, by the way, are relatively inexpensive, say around £3 or £4 per person. They are excellent but cannot go far in a world competition. I am speaking of the little restaurants, modest ones like *Agut* in Barcelona (with the best fish done in light oil), nicely Basque such as *Nicolasa* in San Sebastian, or the picturesque *Botin* in Madrid (with their young eel and their amazing sucking pig baked in an old clay oven) or even like *Mestre Zé*, on the banks of the Tagus near Lisbon, where the crayfish and the chickens with pimento are better than anywhere in the world. In these little

Spanish and Portuguese restaurants it is hard to spend more than about thirty or thirty-five shillings a head.

CM: Be serious. As far as Mediterranean-style food is concerned, you know very well that Italy has the best.

HG: For you, perhaps, but I don't have a single exciting memory. Except for the scampi in *Harry's Bar* in Venice.

CM: And also the *hors d'œuvre* and fillet of beef in *Antico Martini*, the risotto in *Cipriani*. And in Rome, the extraordinary *bollito misto*, a simple dish if ever there was one, in the *Piccolo Mondo*; the stuffed pigs' feet in *Toscana Mario*; the ham in *Flavia*. In Verona, at the *Dodici Apostoli*, the chicken in cream sauce. In Florence, the tripe at *Sabatini*; in Bologna, the truffled pork shoulder at the *Tre Vecchi*; the pigs' feet of the remarkable *Fini* in Modena. And in Milan? Isn't *Giannino* a very great restaurant, even if it's not very intimate?

HG: You always mention one or two dishes. One good dish doesn't make a great restaurant.

CM: At *Giannino's*, I could name twenty. At any rate, with the *antipasto*, which must be the best in the world, the pheasant pâté with truffles, the veal rolled with white truffles or the dorade with shellfish sauce and the coffee tart, you will have a meal that can be equalled only rarely in France.

HG: We've done it! Unless you think that Switzerland is worth a detour. As far as I'm concerned, I quite like *Euler* in Basel, but that's not worth a detour. Just as everywhere else in Switzerland, they cook in the French manner, adequately, but without spark, and that simply isn't worth while.

CM: It's the same in the *Plat d'Argent* in Geneva, the *Lausanne Palace*, the *Grappe d'Or* and the *Beau Rivage* in Lausanne, the *Ascot* in Zurich, to name the best I know. Good, we have gone round the world before starting on France. Let's recapitulate. North America: we'll take *La Crémaillère*, *La Grenouille*, the *Caribbean Room*, *Bardet*, *La Saulaie* and the *Imperial Palace*, Chinese.

HG: In the Far East it's much harder. Let's keep the *Siamese Birdsnest* in Hong Kong – even though I have had only one meal there, that one was extraordinary. In Africa, your *Maison Arabe*.

CM: *Dronningen* in Norway, *La Vallée* in Belgium, *Giannino* in Italy.

HG: That makes six restaurants for the rest of the world to face France, and it will be easy to choose at least as many from France. You start.

CM: It's *not* easy. Are we going to choose the great ones, the middle, the small ones? *Les Lyonnais*, for example, in Paris is nothing more than a bistro. But it is one of the greatest restaurants in France for anyone who likes bistro cuisine.

HG: Absolutely. And it is one restaurant where I have *never* been disappointed.

CM: But there are an infinite number of bistros in Paris and the provinces. On the other hand, we are not going to reject all the

110

great luxury restaurants because they are too well known, too famous for their great cuisine, too expensive. Well, we'd better dive in. In Paris: luxury, *Lucas-Carton*; small de luxe restaurant, *Chez Denis*; bistro, *Les Lyonnais*; suburbs, *Le Vieux Marly*. In the provinces, *Troisgros* and *Bocuse* (near Lyons), the Haeberlin brothers' *Auberge de l'Ill* in Illhaeusern (Alsace), the *Poste* in Avalon (Burgundy), *Barrier* in Tours (Loire), *L'Oasis* in La Napoule (Côte d'Azur). Beyond these, I'm at sea. There are too many, great or small.

HG: It's a choice, of course, and I share it, except perhaps *L'Oasis*, which is excellent but not up to this level. But you have cheerfully forgotten *Lasserre, La Tour d'Argent, Le Grand Véfour, Maxim's, Le Petit Bedon, Allard, Garin, Jamin, L'Ami Louis, La Marée* and a number of others in Paris. As for the provinces, obviously we must consider the case of *Père Bise* at Talloires. . . . Not to mention Mme Point's *Pyramide* at Vienne, *Baumanière* at Baux de Provence, the *Club* at Cavalière, Puget's *Le Petit Brouant* at Nice, *Rostang* at Sassenage, *Hiély* at Avignon, *Le Chapon Fin* at Thoissey.

CM: I haven't forgotten them, I'm lost. Once more, everything depends on what you call a very good restaurant: must it first and foremost be dependable in quality? Then I agree that *Lasserre* and *Pyramide* move to the top. Or have some great specialities? Then I will keep *Lucas-Carton* and his woodcock among my top choices, even if sometimes you do get almost mediocre dishes there. Or then with luck you can sometimes eat something sublime, unforgettable. Then, for the *macaroni au foie gras et à la langouste* I take *Le Grand Véfour*; for its *feuilleté au homard* and its *demoiselles* of venison, *Le Vieux Marly*; for their oysters gratiné, *Le Petit Bedon* and *La Marée*; *Prunier* for the lobster in court bouillon; *Le Vivarois* for the sweetbread tart; *La Mère Michel* for the *beurre blanc*; *Maxim's* for the woodcock and the saddle of veal; *La Tour d'Argent* for the sole stuffed with crayfish, etc. But it's unjust and there's no end to it. And I've only mentioned specialities in Paris!

HG: Then we must do something drastic. Let's each name three. For me, I name . . . ah . . . I name *Bocuse, Troisgros, Denis*. That's it, *Denis*.

CM: I'll go along with that. For me, it is *Troisgros, Bocuse* and . . . I don't know. *Haeberlin? Lucas-Carton? Denis*, perhaps, in the end. But *Denis* is surely mad.

HG: Yes, he's mad. And a madman can't represent France in an international contest.

CM: We had better explain to our readers what we mean by mad.

❀ ❀ ❀ ❀ ❀ ❀ ❀ ❀ ❀

PARIS Ⓟ 75. ㊏, ⑩. G. Paris – 2 607 625 h. Alt. Observatoire 60, pl. Concorde 34.

Aérogare, 2 r. Constantine, esplanade Invalides (7ᵉ) ☎ 468.96.20.

※※※ ❀ **Chez Denis** (fermé du 22 juil. au 12 sept., sam. et dim. de Pâques à Pentecôte et lundi toute l'année), 10 r. Gustave-Flaubert ☎ 924.40.77, Rep carte 40 à 72 ▮8.
Spéc. : Homard bordelaise, Foie gras d'oie frais, Agneau gratin dauphinois – 🍷. 🦐.

○ **ROANNE** ◁❂▷ 42 Loire. ⑦③-⑦ – 54 748 h. Alt. 279 – **Exc.** : S : Gorges de la Loire★ par D 56 (AZ) 3 – ☊Ⓓ⊐ – **S.I.,** A.C. et T.C.F. cours République ☎ 71.51.77.
Paris 389 ⑥ – Charolles 59 ① – Lyon 87 ③ – Mâcon 97 ① – Moulins 98 ⑥ – St-Étienne 78 ⑤ – Thiers 60 ④ – Vichy 74 ⑥ – Villefranche-sur-Saône 76 ③.

※※※ ❀ ❀ **Troisgros** (fermé du 2 au 9 janv.) (avec ch.), pl. Gare ☎ 71.26.68, Rep 6. 35/55 et carte ▮5. Spéc. : Mousse de grive au genièvre, Escalope de saumon Troisgros (fév.-sept.), Pièce de Charollais au Fleurie à la moelle. Vins : Fleurie, Fuissé – **19 ch** 49/85 stc – 🐟 🅱 (rest)
🍷 🚰wc. . . . . AY 𝐫

❀ ❀ ❀ ❀ ❀ ❀ ❀ ❀ ❀

○ **LYON** Ⓟ 69 Rhône. ⑦⑩-⑩⑫ – 535 000 h. Alt. 169 – ☊Ⓓ⊐

Paris 459 ⑩ – Aix-les-Bains 112 ④ – Annecy 145 ④ – Besançon 208 ① – Chambéry 112 ④ – Clermont-Fd 179 ⑨ – Dijon 198 ⑩ – Genève 156 ③ – Grenoble 105 ④ – Marseille 323 ⑥ – Moulins 185 ⑥ – Nice 472 ⑥ – St-Étienne 56 ⑦ – Valence-sur-Rhône 101 ⑥ – Vichy 161 ⑨.

A Collonges-au-Mont-d'Or (9 km par N433 et D 51 – GR) – ✉ Collonges-au-Mont-d'Or :

※※※ ❀ ❀ **Paul Bocuse** (fermé du 4 au 24 août), 50 quai Plage (au pont) ☎ 47.00.14 « Élégante installation » Rep 45/55 et carte Spéc. : Pâté Pantin Ferdinand Wernert, Mousse de truite à la Constant Guillot, Carré d'agneau à la broche. Vins : Pouilly-Fuissé, Brouilly – 🍷. Ⓟ.

In his case to be mad means to refuse to pay any attention to the imperatives of his profession: costs, for example. He buys the most expensive things, invents dishes such as his *brouillade* (brains and sweetbreads, lobster, truffles, sauce Cardinal!) which he cannot serve for less than £6, has built a seawater pond for his oysters, and raises his own crayfish, refuses to serve anyone who just drops in,

112

demands that you drink wines that are up to the standard of his dishes, loses his temper with guests who do not know that duck should be eaten while it is still bloody – he's right a thousand times – searches out and prepares long-forgotten recipes and is amazed that at the price he charges (a good £8 or £9 per person) he hardly ever has any customers. But he persists in remaining the costly, proud saint of French cuisine. To be mad, in his case, means to deny the sad realities of his profession. It will kill him.

HG: Don't forget that *Troisgros* and *Bocuse* would also be considered mad if they were not in the provinces and thus often can produce meals for half what they would cost in Paris.

CM: *Troisgros* in particular. These two brothers and their father do things that no one in the world can do any more. Because the neighbourhood boys supply them with crayfish they catch with a net and a lamb's head, just as in the old days, or frogs trapped with a red rag, or snails that come out after the rain. Their beef comes from a meadow in Charolais, quite near, and they select it practically on the hoof. They shoot their young partridge themselves. The winegrowers bring them new wine on the sly, from the best vats. They *live* their cuisine daily, playing with it like children, while they are the greatest chefs in the world.

HG: Ah, you have tipped your hand. You prefer the *Troisgros*. They are your final choice.

CM: Not necessarily. I like *Bocuse* as well as you do.

HG: But perhaps not as well as *Troisgros*. I readily admit that the *Troisgros'* cuisine is more simple, less sophisticated, more likely to appeal to the humble. . . .

CM: Fool, it's just the opposite. It is when you are used to the ostentation of what the Americans call haute cuisine that you are capable of discerning the more delicate charms of the simple and true cuisine.

HG: Which means that *Bocuse* does not produce 'true' cuisine?

CM: Of course he does, but in the image of the person: a great performer, full of personality.

HG: You're right, and that's why I find that his cuisine has more personality, more grandeur, even if every now and then it is overdone. But you will agree that his green bean salad, his mushrooms sautéed in butter, his peaches in Burgundy, are simplicity itself. And they are fabulous! But that he is also creative, that he has imagination, to that I say bravo! His mussel soup with fresh saffron, his partridge *aux choux* without partridge and without butter (the butter is replaced by foie gras and the partridge by the

113

juice of a pressed partridge), his tremendous 'wooden leg soup' (a gigantic *pot au feu* with shins of beef, chicken, partridge, veal, celery, turnips, onions, carrots and seasonings), they are really great, even if not simple. And then his élan, his generosity – the Troisgros have it too, but theirs is more tender, more familial – that taste for the lordly gesture, they belong to a master.

CM: Don't put words into my mouth, Bocuse, at the age of forty-three, is in fact already a master, following the line of Point and Escoffier. Perhaps even a greater master. But in the end what makes me prefer the Troisgros a little is exactly that they are not working for glory, they don't act like geniuses and they are geniuses nevertheless. One is Shakespeare, the others are Molière.

HG: Perhaps in fact it is a difference of this sort that separates them and reunites them at the summit. And it is good that France can present these two expressions, the one of glory, the other of wisdom, of the great cuisine. To compete with whom, by the way?

HG: The Troisgros brothers and Bocuse against – the Chinese chef at the *Imperial Palace*?

CM: The Moroccan cooks of the *Maison Arabe*? I think this little game will win us the title of 'the world's two most ridiculous gourmets'.

ADRIAN MITCHELL

Gastronomic Pornography

Anchovies in aspic
With marinated aubergines.
Beetroot bellies in brandy
With a bucket of Heniz Baked Beans.
Alligator puree and I don't care
If you stuff it with reindeer rind,
But gastronomic pornography
Is booting me out of my mind.

Cavair and cakemix
Makes coriander chocolate cheese.
Chutneyed carrots and coffee –
Won't you slice me a doorstep please?
Pass me down a mousse with its antlers on
You can cook it in fairy snow,
For gastronomic pornography
Is dragging me down so low.

Gammon stuffed with garlic,
Geraniums and gooseberry fool.
Grouse, gazpacho and ginger,
Burn your kitchen and leave to cool.
I want Mrs Beeton to be my man
And Elizabeth David too,
For gastronomic pornography
Makes my stomach feel like a zoo.

HUGH JOHNSON

Confessions of a Merman

OMETIMES I THINK
I must be a merman,
and a half-cannibal one at that, to enjoy browsing on the sea bed
as much as I do. I remember a particular *plat de fruits de mer* at
Honfleur which was quite simply that: a bare-handed predator's
banquet on all the stony, scaly or limpid beasts that lie, crawl, or
proceed in illogical little flicks among the wrack and the wrecks,
stirring up the sand or disguised as pebbles.

There were shrimps and oysters, whelks and mussels, winkles and
cockles and clams. The napkins were sea-green with crustaceous
designs. The plate was virtually a bivalve in pottery. The wine,
palest green from a dark green bottle, was as cold and as tangy,
almost, as the sea itself.

The toss of a lobster-pot from the harbour wall, where pyramids
of tarry rigging were black against the moon, the café-restaurant
Aux Deux Ponts was like an extension of the sea bed, with the only
difference that the water boiled. I returned there with unabated
appetite for grilled sole, steamed turbot, moules mariniéres night
after night.

The sea-food passion to me is a peculiarly holiday thing. I will,
admittedly, nip into an oyster bar before the theatre, or revel in a
big brown Dover sole at any time. But the fish-net nauticality of
most inland fish restaurants, whether Frying Tonite or Prunier's,
holds no magic for me.

It is the sight of a tubby little fishing boat, and the smell, stale

and fresh at the same time, on the jetty, which starts the craving for fish, fish, fish, fish (as Fats Waller put it), fish.

I won't say that all the beckoning quay-side cafés come up to expectation. Bergen was a bad let-down. My fault, no doubt, for letting the guide-book persuade me for a moment that boiled cod could be worth trying. The place was as tarry as can be. Upstairs, one felt, there could only be a sail-loft. But the jug of melted butter which we were relying on to gild a most unhappy monochrome of cod and potatoes, both boiled, turned out to be margarine. . . .

Then there was the restaurant at Juneau, Alaska, where an enormous and wholly delicious slice of King Salmon (the beast in question had weighed almost 100 pounds and the slice was in proportion) was presented with *spaghetti bolonaise* on the side. And on the other side, as it were, roaring hot mama belting out *The Lady is a Tramp* to a growling cornet.

The search for fish has taken me to some curious places. The struggle to photograph it – I have what I am told is an unusual

118

urge to photograph fish before I dispatch it – has led me into even odder ones. How should I have explained to the lady beside whom on the park bench the struggling lobster landed, out of a clear sky, feet upwards, that I had only poured a jug of water over it on its dish on the balcony above because the sun had dried its shell to a dull brown – in Portuguese?

The great thing is, though, that I have established some real favourites. I can remember every detail of a good half dozen of fish restaurants with considerable pleasure. Aux Deux Ponts at Honfleur is one – though one of the simplest. Another, right at the other end of Normandy – in fact just in Picardy – is the much better known Chez Mado at Le Crotoy.

Chez Mado is just across from the jetty where Mado's boats bring Mado's fish to land. Madame Mado Poncelet, when not slipping out to Mass in her red two-seater and her Pucci shirt, presides in a house where they might have stopped the Creation at Day Two.

From the delicate pink mounds of shrimps which appear beside your aperitif to the moment when you feel you were jolly lucky not to get lobster coffee you are subjected to the fruits of the Channel – and more particularly the bay of the Somme – without respite.

When breakfast comes up to your room and the shutters are thrown back, you are just in time to see the night's catch chugging by to the jetty. Before you turn in you will watch the boxes of flapping silver from another expedition being swung ashore.

At Chez Mado they cook with cream, as they do in all of Normandy and most of its neighbour regions. The address of her establishment, which is particularly handy for travellers who use Le Touquet airport, is Hôtel de la Baie, Le Crotoy, Somme.

My other favourite which is really down among the fishing boats is actually on the beach. The whole restaurant has sand between its toes, being an open-sided platform, roofed with matting, jutting out among the dinghies hauled above high water.

Casa Juan has one of the hardest reputations to acquire: a reputation among wine-shippers – for its beach is at Sanlucar de Barrameda where manzanilla, the driest of sherries, is made. From Casa Juan you look across the Guadalquivir estuary to the strange, deserted wild-life sanctuary of the Coto Doñana.

At table there you eat the world's best gambas (giant prawns), grilled red mullet so tiny that you pick them up and swallow them, head and all, like whitebait, and delicious tender octopus. Moreover there is a wine on the list which is seen, to the best of my knowledge, nowhere else; a manzanilla amontillado – dark, dry, and as soft and strong as any number of things I can think of but daren't mention.

I'm not sure whether a riverine fish restaurant really counts. It does for me in the case of El Vaticano, whose river, the Hispano Portuguese border, the Minho, is to little eels what the straits of Dover presumably are to soles.

In the lamprey season, in April, good eel-eaters come from all over Portugal – which means, make no mistake, Mozambique and Angola as well – to eat little lampreys cooked *en brioche,* stewed in red wine, or served in a particularly saucy dish with lots of pepper. Before going on, let me add, to roast kid, ewe's milk cheese, and bowls of exotic, Portuguese-African fruit. The address of this simple, cheap but distinguished house is El Vaticano, Moncao, Minho, Portugal.

One can roam Europe in this way, picking on places where the fish is excellent in itself, and memorable in the way it is served. Dubrovnik has excellent fish restaurants, slightly forbidding in appearance but uniformly good.

Venice is rather disappointing. The Piraeus is a better place to look than Athens. Marseilles has made such a thing of it that quality has suffered. Barcelona has such greedy citizens that all is well.

Only one complaint is universal, in my experience. And this seems a good place to air it. There is an international shell-fish ring at work, which sees to it that anything from a Dublin Bay prawn to an out-and-out lobster costs a small fortune wherever you buy it.

You can wade out into the surf to meet the fisherman and still pay almost what you would pay at Wheeler's. I have heard of honest tars parting with a lobster for half-a-quid but I have never seen one. Not that I let it spoil my shell-fish pleasure.

A Celebration o

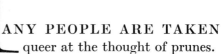

MANY PEOPLE ARE TAKEN
queer at the thought of prunes.
Such prune-haters should be converted; they should be purged of
the stewed-prune memories of childhood, the prune being an

ingredient necessary to some of the best meat and fish dishes ever devised. (I can think of only one way in which prunes should not be eaten – and that is *à l'anglaise*, stewed in too much water and served with custard-powder sauce or with rice pudding.)

I confess to having been a prune-hater myself until recently. Once school days were past, I sedulously avoided prunes for the next twenty years. Then under the douce influence of Touraine, Henry James's succulent and good-humoured land, I began to recognise the excellence of these winter fruit, prepared so lovingly from the swollen purple Agen plums of August. I began to have a regard for their richness, which marries so well with wine in the pork, rabbit and eel dishes of the Loire country.

Our finest prunes have come for centuries from France, as their name indicates, *prune* being the French for plum, but France is not their homeland. One legend claims that improved plums were only introduced into France from Italy in the 1400s by René, king of the two Sicilies, duke of Anjou, and count of Provence. Already Italian plums had a long pedigree, thanks to those excellent gardeners the Romans. They had taken and developed many varieties of their own, for eating fresh and for drying, from the Middle East, which is the true ancestral home of all our modern plums. The only souvenir we have retained in England of this source is the name damson, a corruption of Damascene, meaning of or from Damascus. Here is another souvenir, a more modern one, from that area – I recommend it not entirely out of piety, as you will see when you taste it:

Pour boiling hot tea over 1lb prunes, and leave overnight. Next day remove the stones, replacing them by shelled walnuts (fresh walnuts are particularly good for this dish). Fit the stuffed prunes neatly into a large saucepan. Bring ½pt of the tea in which the prunes soaked to the boil, with 2 heaped tablespoons of sugar and 1 tablespoon lemon juice. Pour it over the prunes, simmer them for half an hour and put the pan aside to cool. Arrange the prunes in a shallow serving dish, with a little of the syrup. Beat up together ¼pt each double and single cream with a little sugar. Cover the prunes with the whipped cream, and chill well before serving.

I should like to be able to associate plums and prunes with such a man as King René, who had feelings and intelligence of a kind not normally associated with monarchs. I should like to think he encouraged the prune industry of Touraine, so near to his castle of Angers. He did not, however, plant the first plum orchards at Agen, much farther south, upstream from Bordeaux, where a special plum was developed centuries ago, probably by monks, a plum particularly good for drying. This Prune d'Agen is large and very sweet; moreover, it has the desirable quality of not falling off

124

the tree the moment it is ripe. It stays on the branch to acquire a few days' extra sweetness, then falls obligingly into the picker's hand the moment it is touched. (Other kinds of plum recommended for drying are the Perdrigons, or our own Ickworth Imperatrice, developed by Thomas Knight the great fruit grower in the early nineteenth century. When housewives in this country were accustomed to preparing their own prunes, they would use St Catherine plums, or St Julien, or Black Diamond, or Fellenberg plums, which are of Italian origin.)

When the plums are picked, they are dipped for half a minute or less in boiling water (or a weak soda solution). This removes some of the waxiness, and cracks the skin with a fine network of lines. Then they are laid in the sun to dry, either out of doors or under glass. Should the sun not maintain the usual ardour of an Agenais summer, the plums will be transferred to drying tunnels, where blasts of air at 160° will complete the process. Some plums dry out more than others: this does not matter, as moisture content evens out when the prunes are jammed tightly together in packages.

This is the method of manufacture in a good climate such as the south-west of France or Provence or Italy (or California, where, in an even more reliably dry climate, the plums can be left to fall off the tree, so that they achieve the maximum sweetness possible). Further north, in Touraine, an excellent if less famous prune country, one may sometimes see relics of an older method of artificial drying. Walking along a sunken lane in that unpeopled, yet gentle countryside, one often comes to a hamlet of caves warrening an exposed rock face. In front of them a walnut tree or two survives, a bay tree, some apple trees and a medlar. The plum trees have gone. The caves are now barred with strong doors, shutting in a thousand bottles of wine, the pressoir and the great barrels. No families live there any more; no smoke comes from the chimneys which poke up from the slopes of the cliff top on the edge of the vines. The only hint of past existence is a blackened flare of rock, above a hole gaping at waist-height, beside one of the cave doors. A child might crawl into this minuscule cave, this old horseshoe-shaped oven cut into the rock. Fifty years ago the fallen bricks would have been beautifully ranged to line the oven. One imagines the wives of the hamlet baking their bread, then quickly laying the wicker trays of plums in the slowly dying heat to dry. Next day the process would be repeated, and the day after. When the plums had wrinkled from purple to black, they would be packed in layers with bay leaves tucked in between. (One still sees the beautiful round wicker-trays with their low rim – cheeses are put on them to finish when they are past the dripping stage, cakes at the bakery are displayed on them, or fish in the market.)

Such prunes were often added to harsh locally distilled *marc*, to soften the flavour. A more elegant recipe instructs one to put 1lb of unsoaked prunes into a 2-pint bottling jar, with 18 lumps of sugar dissolved in a scant $\frac{1}{4}$pt of boiling water. Then fill the jar up with Armagnac, and leave for six weeks. The prunes are served in tiny glasses with a little of the liqueur. Very good.

I should like to have tasted those bread-oven prunes of Touraine when they were combined with local white wines. Particularly with the white wines of Vouvray, made from grapes so ripe that 'they piss in your hand', as the locals say, when you pick them. This late *vendange* tests the nerve and judgement of the *vigneron*, but he has his reward.

PORC AUX PRUNEAUX DE TOURS is the right dish to eat with such wines:

    30 prunes, soaked overnight in $\frac{1}{2}$ bottle Vouvray
    4 thick pork loin chops, boned; seasoned flour
    2oz butter; dessertspoon redcurrant jelly
    $\frac{1}{2}$pt thick cream; lemon juice, salt, pepper

Turn the chops in seasoned flour, and fry in butter on both sides until golden. Add 2–3 tablespoons of the Vouvray in which the prunes soaked, cover the pan and simmer for 30 minutes. Meanwhile cook the prunes in another pan in their wine. Put meat and drained prunes when cooked on to a hot serving dish and keep them warm. Pour the remains of the prune liquid into the pork juices and boil down to a syrup. Stir in the redcurrant jelly until dissolved, then add the cream gradually to bind the sauce. Season with lemon juice, salt and pepper. Pour over pork and prunes and serve immediately.

Pork with prunes is no monopoly of Touraine. In the eighteenth century Goldsmith remarked that pig with prune sauce is very good eating to a hungry man. He would not have been thinking of the French style of cream sauce, but something more like this American prune sauce for eating with pork, smoked ham and so on:

    8oz dried prunes
    1 teaspoon cornflour; 2 tablespoons brown sugar
    $\frac{1}{4}$ teaspoon salt; lemon juice
    4 dessertspoons sweet sherry

126

Soak, cook in water to cover, and chop the prunes. Discard the stones. Take about ½pt of the prune cooking liquor and thicken it with cornflour. Simmer for 10 minutes with sugar, salt and lemon juice to taste. Just before serving add the chopped prunes to heat through, and the sherry.

American cookery books are full of prune recipes, a reflection of the enormous prune production of California these days. A Frenchman grew the first Pruneaux d'Agen there in the middle of the last century, by 1900 the industry produced 140 million pounds a year: nowadays the average is 340 million pounds. Although the true Agen prunes have the reputation, and are the doyens undoubtedly of the industry, it would be an unwise person who could claim to tell the difference between Agen prunes from Agen and Agen prunes from the Santa Clara valley of California. One might conclude from other kinds of experience that the largest prunes must be American, but in a *matelotte* of eel or a bowl of cocky leeky, both kinds exude their richness with a fine equality. In fact it was reported early this century, in 1905, that French prune-packers were known to have imported Californian prunes, repackaged them, and sold them back to the Americans as Pruneaux d'Agen. Which of course they were – botanically speaking.

Along with other dried fruit, prunes have been imported into this country since the Middle Ages. They were welcome in wintertime when fruit was short, and were regarded as something of a luxury. At Christmas they went into plum porridge, the precursor of Christmas plum pudding which did not make its appearance until the seventeenth century. Other ingredients were tongue, suet, raisins, spices, wine, and breadcrumbs. By the mid-eighteenth century, plum pudding and sweet meat mixtures not unlike medieval plum porridge belonged also to harvest time, the other great season of the year for celebration. Reapers were hired for a month's work, and if the farmer didn't provide plum pudding to follow pickled pork and boiled beef, he was liable to find it difficult to hire the best men the following year. One writer on farmhouse economy suggested that raisins should be substituted for prunes, or plums as he called them: they would go farther and cost less. Goodbye to the plums in plum pudding. But he did suggest that one use for prunes, when their expense was justified, was to disguise the flavour of tainted meat. If the mutton or beef was chopped small, and stewed with prunes, raisins, spices, and brown sugar, and covered with a crust, no one would be any the wiser.

128

So the English misuse of prunes goes back quite a long way. I prefer to think of COCKY LEEKY with prunes, a dish claimed by the Scots now, but once eaten elsewhere in Britain:

1lb prunes; 1 capon, chicken or boiling fowl
2–3lb leeks; beef stock

Soak the prunes overnight. Next day fit the bird, breast down, into a pot which just holds it comfortably. Cover with beef stock and bring slowly to the boil. Prepare and slice the leeks, adding half of them to the pot when it has been skimmed. Simmer until the bird is almost cooked (time from 1 to 5 hours according to age). Correct the seasoning, add the prunes stoned, and the rest of the leeks. Cook for another 20 minutes.

If this dish sounds barbaric, remember that it was greatly appreciated by Talleyrand, the French foreign minister (and gourmet). He thought that the prunes should be removed before serving. But this is a shame, because although most of their flavour has been absorbed by the soup, they look so beautiful against the green of the leeks and the pale flesh of the chicken.

Another use for prunes with poultry is to stuff them, soaked but uncooked, into the Christmas turkey or goose or chicken. They can be combined with a sausage-meat stuffing or chestnut stuffing, or simply mixed with quartered apples in the Danish style. But I think the best way is to soak the prunes overnight in half-water and half-red wine, then to simmer them in their soaking liquor, and to stuff them with minced lean pork fried with onion and garlic in a little butter. This mixture should be seasoned well with thyme and spices, and a few chopped olives, and then bound with beaten egg. Refrigerate the stuffed prunes overnight before putting them into the goose or turkey.

There are many other good recipes for stuffed prunes, both savoury and sweet, but the aristocrats of the species are undoubtedly the *pruneaux fourrés* of Tours. These delectable sweets are made by different confectioners of the town (no large factory, no conveyor belt), and I was lucky enough to be able to hear about them from Madeleine Sabat, one of the proprietors of the Maison Sabat in the main street of Tours. We sat and talked one afternoon in the elegant tea shop, with its counters of superb confectionery, and cakes of a kind we rarely see in England. She showed me the three varieties of *pruneaux fourrés* that her brother makes – the oldest kind of all, the traditional *pruneau noir* stuffed with a *purée* of prunes and rum (the favourite with local gourmets), another kind stuffed with a rich orange-coloured apricot and kirsch *purée*, and finally prunes stuffed with a pale green almond and kirsch paste the colour of almonds in their summer skins. They were neatly arranged in rows in little hampers – their design has an air of the early nineteenth century – which are made at Vilaine, a village long famous for basketry. Mlle Sabat told me that Vilaine being near the old plum-growing centre of Huismes, a basket industry grew up there to provide hampers for the prune-packers. Nowadays the young craftsmen of Vilaine are seduced by the profits to be made from fashionable wicker furniture, from chairs, trolleys, linen-baskets, hatstands, screens, and so on. Only the old ladies, the eighty-year-olds, still bother to make these charming little baskets, which will be displayed handsomely in the most elegant confectionery of Tours. Even in the clear air of Touraine, old ladies do not live for ever, and soon it will be all paper boxes.

Another sad thing is that the prunes themselves are no longer from Huismes, or from any other Touraine village, but from Agen so much further south. And I noticed, as I walked into one or two grocers' shops after visiting the Maison Sabat, that most packages of ordinary, uncooked prunes on sale were not even from Agen – but from the Santa Clara valley of California.

PRUNEAUX FOURRÉS DE TOURS

1lb large prunes, soaked and pitted
Almond filling
8oz sugar; $\frac{1}{4}$ gill water; 4oz ground almonds; kirsch
Few drops of green colouring (optional)
Prune or apricot filling
4oz prunes or apricots, unsoaked
About 4oz sugar; rum or kirsch
Syrup
8oz sugar; $\frac{1}{2}$ gill water

Leave the soaked and pitted prunes on a rack in a warm kitchen.

To make the almond filling, bring sugar and water to the soft ball stage. Pour in the almonds, remove from heat; beat until cold (an electric beater helps), adding kirsch to taste, and just enough green colouring to make the mixture a delicate green. Knead on icing-sugar-coated formica or marble surface, until you have a nice coherent ball of marzipan.

130

To make the fruit *purées*, cover apricots or prunes with water and cook slowly until they begin to be soft. Drain and weigh (discard the prune stones first). Add about half the weight of fruit in sugar, and blend in a liquidiser (or sieve). If the mixture sticks in the blender, add a very little of the cooking liquor: cook the fruit a little longer in the first place if you have to sieve or mouli it. Transfer the *purée* to a heavy pan, and cook it slowly over a steady heat until it dries to a very thick mass. Extra sugar may be added to taste, but these *purées* should not be oversweetened, and finally the rum or kirsch. Leave to cool.

To fill the prunes, roll the almond paste into fat nuggets and fold the prunes round them, so that the filling shows well against the dark prune. Make two or three light indentations at a slant across the filling.

The fruit *purées* are stickier and more difficult to handle than the almond paste. At the Maison Sabat they are piped into the prunes with a forcing bag; but you could also roll teaspoons of the *purée* lightly in caster sugar before fitting them into the prunes.

Bring the syrup to the hard ball stage, and have ready a lightly oiled rack. Quickly dip the prunes into the syrup, and leave them on the rack to drain. This makes them shiny. It also makes them sticky, and they need to be packed into tiny paper cases before being handed round. (A larding needle makes a good spear for dipping the prunes into the syrup. Or use a chip basket if you are making them in quantity.)

E. S. TURNER

Petit

Tour

de

France

O MICHELIN, cherish
   Me, chasten and guide me!
And let me not perish
   With songbirds inside me
On the beaches of D-Day,
Sans bain and *sans bidet.*

The Chiribim
Is *fermé dim.*,
   And cannot mend a *pneu.*
The Oriflamme
Is *fermé sam.*,
   But offers *truite au bleu.*

The brasserie
Of Tante Julie
Is *interdit*
   Aux chiens.
Le Chat Qui Chante
Lacks *eau courante –*
   Tiens!

The Auberge Bon Accueil
Has *volaille demi-deuil,*
   Whatever that is,
   With *parking* gratis.

The Chez Dumas (good Chez Dumas!)
Bans TV *pendant les repas.*
The Chez Ron-ron (petit pat-a-pon)
Is *fermé jeudi, hors saison.*
It's *convenable*, with *douche publique*,
But scarcely, it would seem, unique.

The Château Cavour
   On its elegant *plage*
Is worth *le détour,*
   But not worth *le voyage.*

Behold, *enfin,*
The Vieux Moulin
Has *matelote de Rhin*
Au vin,
And, furthermore, *un beau jardin*
To rest in after such *délices*
As *gratin de queues d'écrevisses,*
Or *langouste grillé cardinal,*
Which sounds a long way from banal.

O scene
   Of high-class nutriment!
My pulse beats plus fifteen
   Per cent.

What of the Cochon Noir?
It's *fermé trois prem, sem.*
   d'août et lundi soir.

The Lion d'Or is *isolé,*
With *nombre de couverts limité;*
It boasts *terrine de caneton*
Au foie gras truffé . . . Zut, mais non!

I suddenly feel queasy.
Let's take it easy.

Right here I say
   Farewell, *mon cher,*
To *fricassée*
   De fruits de mer.
Farewell to *lamproie bordelaise*
(Or *lyonnaise* or *béarnaise*),
Goodbye to *gratin dauphinois*
And all *grillades au feu du bois;*
   I'd HATE
   A plate
Of *petits pois.*

I think I'd like – the way things are –
A sandwich at the Buffet Gare
De St. Lazare.

ANTHONY POWELL

Remembrance of Meals Past

SHOULD PREFER
glycerine – yes, hot, excellent.'
Marcel, dining with Saint-Loup in a Paris restaurant rather later
than usual one foggy night, was horrified to hear these words
spoken by a guest sitting behind him, instead of what was apparently the most normal order: 'Bring me a wing of chicken and a
glass of champagne – not too dry.'

The statement turned out less daunting than at first appeared,
being merely uttered by a doctor using the first-person singular in
reply to an acquaintance, who, seeing his physician at one of the
tables, had hoped to get some free medical advice. All the same, as
the shadow of the sick-room hangs over so much of *A la Recherche
du Temps Perdu*, one would not be altogether surprised if Marcel
himself had indeed, even if apologetically, made glycerine his
appetiser that evening. *Tisanes* and orangeade were more in his line
than aperitifs and *vin ordinaire*. The gourmet, especially the
amateur of wine, who hopes to be provided by Proust with the same
subtleties on the subject of eating and drinking which he finds
about, say, love, friendship, social life, writing, painting, music,
will be disappointed. Nevertheless, investigation of their treatment
is of interest, even when negative. We may regret that the local
wines of France do not receive the attention devoted to place-
names and their origin, churches and their architecture, but what
is recorded about food and drink is well worth considering. I shall
do no more here than indicate the lines along which an ambitious
student might gain a Ph.D.

136

Glance at Food
and Wine in Proust

The classic mention of wine in the novel is, of course, Swann's gift of Asti Spumante to Marcel's aunts Céline and Flora; his grandfather's uneasiness that these ladies offered no apparent thanks for the present; the aunts' own self-satisfaction in having expressed their gratitude obliquely by reference to 'some people having nice neighbours'. Cyril Ray, in *Through a Glass Lightly*, records his surprise – which many must have shared – that a connoisseur like Swann should have presented an Italian wine, and especially Asti, even to a couple of elderly provincial maiden ladies. Mr Ray goes on to say – quoting among other authorities the *Pink 'Un's* Dwarf of Blood and his collaborator Algernon Bastard in *The Gourmet's Guide to Europe* – that France was then, and still remains, Italy's best customer for sparkling wine. Swann was to be relied upon to produce just what was required, and it would certainly be true to say that Asti has something of its own in bouquet compared with even the sweetest French champagne.

A warning note is struck early in Proust's book by the fact that Marcel's grandfather is not allowed to drink liqueurs. On account of this, his great-aunt – to tease her sister-in-law – used to persuade him to take a few drops of brandy after dinner. This habitually upset Marcel's grandmother. However, the emphasis is on the pain caused to her, rather than on the quality of the brandy, about which we are told no more than that only very little was consumed, and it did not do the slightest harm.

Where food was concerned in Marcel's home at Combray, the presiding genius was their cook Françoise, one of the great figures

of *A la Recherche*. She had come there from Aunt Léonie's, where she played an important rôle in discussing the neighbours, with special reference to such matters as who had been able to buy the largest branches of asparagus. Françoise, like most good cooks, was inclined to become bored with the uneventful routine of family cooking, and *bœuf à la casserole* seems to have been a fairly frequent item on the daily menu. Such humdrum dishes were varied, not only by the march of the seasons, but also by the moods of Françoise herself, who would serve up brill, 'because the fish-woman had guaranteed its freshness'; a turkey, 'because she had seen a beauty in a neighbouring village'; cardoons (a vegetable like the artichoke) with marrow, 'because she had never done them before'; roast leg of mutton, 'because the cold air makes one hungry'; spinach, 'by way of a change'; apricots, 'because they were hard to get'; gooseberries, 'because in another fortnight they would be over'; raspberries, 'which Monsieur Swann had bought specially'; cherries, 'the first to come from the cherry tree which had not yielded for two years'; cream cheese, 'because Marcel was extremely fond of it'; almond cake, 'because she had ordered one the evening before'; *crème chocolat*, 'because it was one of her specialities'.

As a boy at Combray, Marcel was usually sufficiently interested about dinner to go down to the kitchen beforehand to find out what was 'on'. Exciting arrangements of vegetables were always to be found set out there. The kitchen was also, of course, the scene of that 'solemn passover', the servants' mid-day dinner, though this is only referred to after the family had come to live in Paris in the house where they shared a courtyard with the Guermantes. Not even Marcel's father would have dared to ring during the celebration of that sacred congress, and, had he so far forgotten himself as to have done so by mistake, no one would have taken the slightest notice. The rite ended with Françoise undoing the napkin from round her throat, after which she wiped away the last traces of watered wine and coffee. So far as wine went, Françoise would always accept a glass offered between meals from time to time, by Jupien, – not yet revealed to Marcel in his intimate role vis-à-vis Monsieur de Charlus and others – social occasions that also required a longish talk. At those awkward moments when Marcel inadvertently entered the kitchen to find Françoise entertaining her daughter to a complicated spread, this was always designated by her as 'just having a scrap'.

However, the great set-piece for a meal at Marcel's home is

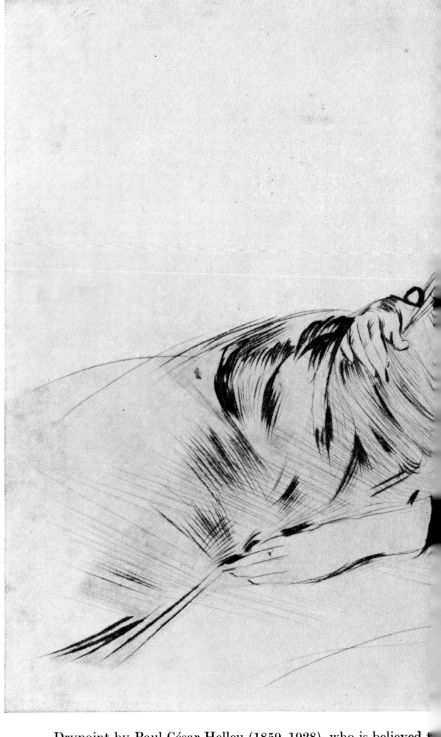

Drypoint by Paul César Helleu (1859–1928), who is believed t

original of Elstir in *A la Recherche du Temps Perdu*

undoubtedly the dinner to which the former Ambassador, Monsieur de Norpois, was invited: partly to advise Marcel on the choice of a career. The *pièce de résistance* was *bœuf en daube*, that is to say cold beef spiced with carrots, 'lodged by the Michael Angelo of our kitchen upon enormous crystals of jelly, like transparent blocks of quartz'. M. de Norpois was delighted with the manner in which the beef was cooked:

'You've a chef in the top class, Madame,' he said. 'That is
not an easy thing to achieve. I myself, when I was living
abroad, had to maintain a certain style in entertaining, and
I know how difficult it is to find a perfect master in the kitchen.
This is a veritable banquet you've set before us.'

M. de Norpois uses the characteristically carefully selected term *agapes*, meaning a love-feast held by the early Christians:

'This is the sort of thing you can't get in a tavern, even
the best of them,' he went on. 'A *daube de bœuf* in which the
jelly doesn't taste of glue and the beef has caught the flavour
of the carrots. It's admirable. Invite me please again.'

At this point he made a sign to show that he wanted more jelly. 'I should be interested to see how your Vatel would manage a dish of a different sort,' he said. 'I should like, for instance, to see him tackle *bœuf stroganoff*.'

Bœuf stroganoff (mushrooms, sour cream, olives, onions, lemon) gives us further insight into M. de Norpois's tastes, though he was not always prepared to reveal these. For example, Marcel's mother was hoping for praise for the pineapple-and-truffle salad, but the Ambassador, 'after fastening on it for a moment the penetrating glance of a trained observer', ate it 'with the inscrutable discretion of a diplomat', without disclosing his opinion. However, a moment later he could not prevent himself from exclaiming: 'What do I see? Nesselrode pudding! After a Lucullan feast of this sort I shall have to take a cure at Carlsbad.'

Afterwards, when congratulating Françoise on the dinner (they never seem to have admitted to M. de Norpois that their cook was a woman), Marcel's mother said: 'The Ambassador assured me that he knows no place where he can get cold beef and *soufflés* such as yours'; so presumably a *soufflé* was also one of the courses of the dinner. It is, however, notable – and very regrettable – that we are told nothing of the wine given to M. de Norpois, who might be expected to rise to great heights of praise or sink to depths of blame, when speaking of vintages he had enjoyed or execrated.

The question why Françoise made better jelly than that supplied at the great restaurants opens up an interesting list of names. Her own explanation of the restaurants' relative failure in this direction was that they 'do it in too much of a hurry', though she was prepared to admit that she could mention 'one of those cafés where they knew a bit about cooking'. The ideal to be aimed at she described as beef that was 'like a sponge' and mopped up the juice. Marcel's father, who had joined the discussion, asked if the restaurant to which Françoise allowed this claim was Henry's in the Place Gaillon, where he regularly attended *repas de corps* – club dinners:

'Oh, no,' said Françoise, evidently feeling some contempt. 'I meant a little restaurant. Henry's is more like a soup-kitchen.'

'Weber's, then?'

'Oh, no, sir, I meant a good restaurant. Weber's, that's in the Rue Royale, that's not a restaurant, it's a *brasserie*. I don't even know if they serve you there. I don't think they have any table-cloths, they just throw it in front of you anyhow.'

'Ciro's?'

'Oh, there I should think the cooking's done by *dames du monde*' – meaning ladies of the *demi-monde* – 'they need that to get the young men in! No, I mean a restaurant where they have a good little *cuisine bourgeoise*. That's what brings the money in. Madame knows it, right along the *grandes boulevardes*, a little way back.'

This restaurant finally turned out to be the Café Anglais.

At about the same period as this, Marcel was receiving invitations to Swann's house, but we are told little about the food there. Odette's anglomania caused her to provide Christmas pudding at the appropriate season, and certainly on one occasion there was lobster *à l'Americaine*. One might have expected here a dissertation on the question whether this manner of cooking had not once been *à l'Armoricaine* – in the Breton way – but Proust does not tackle the issue. Incidentally, in Madame Prunier's Cookery Book, the 'Armorican' version is different from the 'American', though only

very slightly, the sauce of the former being bound with egg yolks and cream before being poured over the lobster.

This brings us to the Grand Hotel at Balbec. Madame de Villeparisis, a great epicure, thought the food there indifferent, although she recommended the oysters, the very thought of which made Marcel feel sick. Among the guests staying at the Grand, with his mistress, was a Frenchman who had proclaimed himself 'king' of one of the Cannibal Islands. His goings-on in general caused a good deal of offence to the more staid residents of the hotel, and, among other things, he always drank champagne at luncheon. On a later visit to the same hotel, Marcel found himself having to cope with the manager, who was famous for his malapropisms. Doing his best to offer everything at his disposal, the manager suggested that he should bring up some of the 'old wine' he had downstairs in a *bourrique* (she-ass), meaning a *barrique* (hogshead). He goes on to explain to Marcel that this wine is 'not Château-Lafite', but is almost as 'equivocal' (meaning 'the equivalent'), and, as it is light, would go well with a fried sole. Although the whole sequence is Proust in one of his knockabout moods, one knows pretty well what the wine would have tasted like.

It was also at the Grand Hotel that Monsieur Nissim Bernard, great-uncle of Marcel's friend Bloch, was 'keeping' one of the waiters. M. Nissim Bernard like to lunch in the dining-room every day and watch the young man rush about with trays, a situation Proust compares to sitting in the front row of the stalls for those having an affair with a ballet-girl. This favourite waiter was only a *commis*, but owing to M. Bernard's influence with the management, was singled out for promotion. At one moment he was offered the job of *sommelier*, but M. Bernard made him refuse that post because its duties meant that too little would be seen of him. Instead of charging about in and out of the kitchen, he would merely have approached each table discreetly with the wine-list. It is good to know that this reckless manner of appointing a wine-waiter was renounced from the start, if even for less than the best of reasons.

When Marcel lunched with Bloch's father, a 'light sparkling wine' was brought in a decanter, which purported to be champagne, but was decidedly not. In fact there seems to have been a strong tendency for champagne, or at least sparkling wine, to have been drunk in the middle of the day, and it seems surprising that the King of the Cannibal Island should have made any impression, good or bad, by doing so. For example, on a day's leave from the garrison at Doncières, when he takes his mistress, Rachel, to Paris for luncheon, Saint-Loup drinks champagne. Indeed, he drinks too much of it, because Rachel irritates him by ogling the other men in the restaurant. Incidentally, at Doncières, the officers' mess was at the Cocq-Hardi; the sergeants', at the Faisan Doré.

Marcel and Saint-Loup also drank champagne when they dined together at Rivebelle, near Balbec. Marcel, forgetting for once his grandmother and her anxieties about his health, apparently drank a lot of beer, as well as the champagne; also some port. The passage describing these potations is obscure, so that one is not absolutely certain that he did not actually add a few drops of port to the beer itself, since he says later that he could hardly taste the port. One hopes – indeed, it is much the most likely – that the figure of speech means merely that the port was taken as a digestive – rather than more normally in France as an aperitif – and that by that time it made little impression. In any case Marcel got rather tight. Here, again, the champagne appears to have been unsatisfactory, for several of the diners sent it away as 'not fit to drink', which for some reason gave positive pleasure to the young waiters.

When Albertine became part of Marcel's life, they used to tour the neighbourhood by car, looking at churches. To refresh themselves while doing this they would stop at farms and buy a bottle of 'calvados or cider'. The cider was always described as non-effervescent, but when opened would usually drench both of them from head to foot. Calvados, one feels, might be a little strong for such outings, and it is no surprise to learn that such powerful liquid restoratives ultimately suggested love-making. For shorter trips on foot from the hotel, they would take a bottle of champagne into the forest, or, on a fine evening, enjoy an alfresco no further away than among the dunes. Albertine was never easy to deal with, and, in spite of Marcel's dislike for oysters, always wanted to eat bivalves when she heard them cried for sale in the street. Marcel felt inclined to say that they would be better at Prunier's, but before he could give any such advice, she was tempted by other street-criers: shrimps, skate, whiting, mussels, mackerel. The vendor of the last of these announced his wares with the cry: '*Il arrive le maquereau!*', which always sent a chill down Marcel's spine – not merely because he disliked that particular fish.

Before we depart from the Grand Hotel, another friend of Marcel's must be called to mind in relation to Proust and wine. This is Monsieur Pierre de Verjus, Comte de Crécy, who turns out in due course to be none other than the former husband of Odette.

Comte de Crécy was of very ancient family, related to the English bearers of that title (possibly the Cressys of Lincolnshire), though the connection is puzzling, as the Count's patronymic is later said to be 'Saylor'. He himself was extremely hard-up, living in fact on a pension paid by Swann. Comte de Crécy was also unusually good company, and, although modest about his own family, a notable authority on local pedigrees, also the gastronomic arts. Accordingly, Marcel used often to invite him as a guest.

The Verjus coat-of-arms, in punning reference to the name (it is not clear where 'Saylor' came in) was *a branch of verjuice slipped and leaved sinople* (one translator renders this in English as *vert*, also meaning green, but Proust writes *sinople*, the rarer and more exotic heraldic term); though Marcel, no doubt rightly, judged that M. de Crécy would not have liked to be given verjuice (extract of sour grapes used for cooking) when asked out to luncheon or dinner. Indeed, so far was that from the case that the Count preferred only the most expensive wines in the list, about which he knew a great deal and for which he possessed a notable capacity. Here a real chance is missed of hearing what M. de Crécy ordered, preferably with the price. The suspicion that Proust himself was not deeply interested in wine is to some extent confirmed by the fact that he thinks it worth mentioning that M. de Crécy made the wine-waiter *chambrer* or *frapper* the wines, if so required, and always specified the date when he ordered port or brandy.

The Verdurins' table will be estimated later, but for the moment they are named only in connection with that party of theirs which Monsieur de Charlus attended as a consequence of his passion for the violinist Morel. M. de Charlus is a dominating figure from whom one might reasonably hope for a strong lead in the matter of wine, as on almost every other subject, but the incident in which he is first mentioned as selecting a drink is not encouraging:

'Have you tasted my orangeade?' Madame Verdurin asked him.

'No, I prefer its neighbour, the strawberry juice,' replied the Baron.

He said this in a voice so high that it once suggested his feminine side, even if the choice of beverage, in some eyes, might not have gone far towards prejudicing a reputation for masculine tastes. However, M. de Charlus somewhat redeems himself from the implication of liking sickly drinks on a subsequent occasion, when

148

he is giving Morel dinner at a little restaurant at Saint-Mars-le-Vêtu on the Normandy coast; no doubt a contrast in price with the *Guillaume le Conquérant* at Dives, which Marcel thought very expensive; an opinion that half a century later I myself saw no reason to disallow. At the restaurant chosen by M. de Charlus the waiter brought them two glasses of frothy liquid:

'But I ordered champagne?' said M. de Charlus.
On this occasion, too, he spoke in an unusually shrill
voice.
'But, sir . . .'
'Take it away, this horror which has no connection with
the worst known champagne. It is the emetic called *cup*, which
is usually made of three strawberries rotting in a mixture of
vinegar and seltzer water.'

M. de Charlus uses the English word 'cup', and he evidently felt strongly about it; as well he might. Later on in the meal he upset the staff of the restaurant again by saying fiercely:

'Ask the head waiter if he has a Bon Chrétien.'
'A good christian, I don't understand.'
'Can't you see we've reached the dessert? It's a pear.'

Morel was as much at sea as the waiter, and the Baron, after quoting the example of various members of the aristocracy who grew prize pears, together with references from Molière on the subject of the same fruit, tried to find out what was available in that line:

'Waiter, have you any Doyennée des Comices?'
'No, sir, there aren't any.'
'Have you Triomphe de Jodoigne?'
'No, sir.'
'Any Virginie-Dallet? Or Passe Colmar? No? Very well,
since you've nothing, we may as well go. The Duchesse
d'Angoulême is not in season yet; come along, Charlie.'

M. de Charlus's preoccupation with Morel eventually involved him in the question of fighting a duel, which, although something of a sham from the start, required a second. The Verdurins' friend, Dr Cottard, who had a great medical reputation, and had treated

Marcel as a boy for his asthma, occupied this rôle. Cottard was, indeed, immensely excited about the duel. When it fizzled out, he and Charlus were left confronting each other with nothing to do but go home. The Baron took Cottard's hand – which filled the Doctor with fear that a sexual assault was about to be made on him – but all M. de Charlus suggested was that they should 'take something' together. 'What used to be called a *mazagran* or a *gloria,* drinks one doesn't find any more, like archaeological curiosities . . . a *gloria* would be distinctly suitable to the place and the occasion.'

A *mazagran* (named after the once famous Café Mazagran) is simply coffee in a glass, but a *gloria* is coffee laced with brandy. Here, we may again invoke Mr Ray, who (in his section referring to 'Irish Coffee', mingled, of course, with whiskey) quotes Eliza Acton's *Modern Cookery* as to how to produce 'Burnt Coffee or Coffee à la militaire (*in France vulgarly called gloria*)'. Miss Acton (1799–1859), daughter of a brewer, which may have directed her mind towards food and drink, first published her *Modern Cookery* in 1845. She is probably better remembered for that work, or her treatise on bread, than for her fugitive poems. She never married, but whilst in Paris became for a time engaged to an officer of the French army, who perhaps taught her the term for – and the method of making – the drink that so much took M. de Charlus's fancy. However, Cottard disappointingly replied that he was President of the Anti-Alcoholic League, and that he could not risk some ass of a country doctor coming past and blaming him for not practising what he preached. In fairness to Cottard, it should be remembered that he had ordered 'no alcohol' for Marcel's asthma, when other practitioners had recommended beer, champagne and brandy to produce 'euphoria'.

We must now return to the Verdurins, whose food and drink, as such, might almost be said to play the predominant part in the book. Madame Cottard, early on, had asked if one of their salads was a 'Japanese salad', but that was a joke with obvious reference to a current play by the younger Dumas. We know that they some-times had bouillabaisse, because Monsieur Verdurin once said that 'the bouillabaisse must not be kept waiting'. Perhaps they rather went in for fish, since one of Monsieur de Cambremer's stock re-marks, when an appropriately large one appeared on the Verdurin table, was to say: 'That fish is a fine animal.' He considered this comment sufficiently amusing and charming to absolve him from ever inviting the Verdurins themselves to eat in his own house.

At one of the Verdurin dinners, the Polish sculptor Viradobetski (who was always called 'Ski' because his name was regarded as too difficult to pronounce) asked: 'What is this pretty coloured thing we are eating?' Madame Verdurin replied that it was strawberry mousse.

'It's rav-ish-ing,' said Ski. 'You ought to open bottles of Château Margaux, Château Lafite, port.'

The thought of this prodigal outlay greatly alarmed Mme Verdurin, who at once pointed out that this reference to wine was a very good joke on Ski's part as he himself never touched alcohol. However, Ski was not to be laughed off as easily as that.

'But not to drink,' he said. 'You shall fill all our glasses. They will bring in marvellous peaches, huge nectarines, set out there against the sunset. It will be as luxuriant as a beautiful Veronese.'

'It would cost almost as much,' murmured M. Verdurin.

'But take away those cheeses with their dreadful colour,' said Ski.

He tried to remove his host's plate, who defended his gruyère with all his might. We must infer from this incident that the Verdurins' wine was nothing very remarkable, perhaps also in short supply. At the same time, in fairness to the Verdurins, the great Goncourt pastiche in which they appear, towards the end of *A la Recherche*, shows them in a rather different light. The reader must make up his own mind as to whether Marcel or the Diarist is to be believed.

Goncourt is fancied as recording that M. Verdurin dropped in to escort him to dinner, mentioning at the same time (something one forgets) that Verdurin was a former critic of *La Revue*, who had written a book on Whistler, and – how very up-to-date – was, or had been, a morphine addict. The 'Venetian' wineglass in front of the Diarist at the dinner table, 'une riche bijouterie de rouge est mise par une extraordinaire Léoville acheté à la vente de M. Montalivet'. Montalivet (1800–1880) was a Minister of Louis-Philippe, who promoted museums and published a book of memoirs. One does not know the precise implications of a Léoville bought at his sale. The immediate thought is that the bottle might have been a bit on the old side, but the question deserves closer study, with more information. It should be borne in mind that the double-edged epithet 'extraordinary' is employed.

The food is described as an 'exquisite repast' and a detailed

151

account is given of the crockery off which it was eaten. The menu appears to have included *foie gras* and turbot – the sauce a 'white sauce', not made like 'flour paste', but with butter 'costing five francs a pound'. When Goncourt remarked that her husband must be very proud of his beautiful china, Mme Verdurin replied in a melancholy tone:

'It's easy to see you don't know him,' she said.
She described him as an absolute maniac, indifferent to these refinements.
'A maniac,' she repeated. 'Absolutely that, who would rather drink a bottle of cider in the rather degraded (*encanaillée*) coolness of a Normandy farm.'

The last two examples I chose of having a drink in *A la Recherche* are 'encanaillés' too, both scenes in houses of ill fame. The first was in the smart brothel a little way up the coast from Balbec, which so impressed strangers by its size and air of convenience that they supposed it would be a good hotel in which to stay. M. de Charlus went there with Jupien to spy on Morel. While he was waiting, a 'clever little lady' was sent to amuse him, and, to prevent her taking off her clothes, Charlus had to buy her champagne at forty francs a bottle. The second incident is when Marcel, quite by chance, found himself in the house of homosexual prostitution run by Jupien during the war; frequented, as it turns out, by M. de Charlus, in his more violently sado-masochistic interludes.

'Could somebody kindly tell me to whom to apply to get a room and have something to drink sent up?' asks Marcel, in all innocence.

After negotiation, the boss appears, carrying coils of ominously heavy chains. Marcel explains that he is not feeling well and would like something to drink. Sinister, even hair-raising, things are being said and done all round. The boss's order is something of an anti-climax. 'Pierrot, go down to the cellar and get some *cassis*. . . .'

Marcel's Paris

Street scenes, cafés, posters, and
an old photograph of the Madeleine and its cabs
not previously published

ABOVE AND OPPOSITE: Jules Cheret

156

ABOVE: Jules Cheret
OPPOSITE: E. Berchmans

Goulash

ONLY THE NOSTALGIA of a million exiles scattered across every continent can account for a strong culinary interest in goulash. In itself, the dish is about as probable a candidate for high honours as our own old-fashioned stewed steak or Lancashire hot-pot. Probably, in the heyday of Empire, men sweltering under tropic suns felt in fantasy cool mists; saw a green landscape in driving rain, or the slate roofs of Yorkshire gleaming black on a sleety morning; while in the crowded kitchen a stew bubbled on the hob in a mouth-watering steam. Basically, goulash is no more esoteric.

There is no doubt that Hungarian exiles close their eyes in Toronto and feel the crackling heat of the midsummer in the oven breath of wind that blows over the Pannonian Plain, the *puszta*. They smell the dry odour of fields of maize, and see in the mind's eye the tall sloping tree-trunk, its length dictated by the depth of the well for which it forms the fulcrum; the rich earth crumbles under the feet in the summer drought; vine-leaves, already turning, rustle around the heavy grapes; a flock of geese cackles and there is an inescapable smell of pigs. On the dusty plain, a herd of unbroken horses wheels in patterns like a dance, and a woman with half-a-dozen petticoats under a dark full skirt straightens up from tending the low paprika vines to shade her eyes against the glaring sun with a hand under her kerchief, and see whether the thunderous noise is from the drumming hoofs, or heralds an approaching storm. As to the Empire-builders, a longing for stewed steak is guesswork, but I do know that Hungarians construct idealised visions of their homeland from far away – and even a few miles is far when the border is closed to them – because I have often seen and heard them do it.

In exile, a little house with a garden becomes a stately mansion, and the country lawyer who was one's father becomes a famous advocate; and so the real, the inimitable goulash, which never tastes the same abroad, becomes an exquisite delicacy.

In fact, it is stew, simply. The word *gulyas* originated in the Magyar language, meaning a herd of oxen; the term transferred itself to the herdsmen and then to the soup-like food they cooked for themselves. For the herds of horses and cattle were driven out on to the plain in the summer and the horse-boys or cow-boys stayed with them, sleeping in small tents or shacks that they built for themselves, and cooking their food in cauldrons over wood fires, suspending the round iron vessel by its handle from a tripod of stout branches or an inclined metal rod stuck in the earth and ending in a hook.

Pepper in these parts is not the tropical black or white pepper we are used to, but dried and powdered paprika skins and seeds. This is the essential characteristic of goulash, and without a generous supply of freshly ground paprika you can forget the whole project. The paprika flourishes best in an extremely dry, Continental climate, growing on a low, bushy vine not unlike a tomato plant. The sweetest of the paprikas is indeed very much like a large tomato, sweet and not at all hot, though with harder flesh and skin. Just as there are various types of beans, so there is a variety of paprikas, though all of the same genus, going from red, through green to yellow in increasing ferocity. The sharpest of all are the long, thin yellow ones. The green and red variety, popular in England and France for salad-making, are relatively mild since they have not been dried, the red version merely being riper. Other types, the long thin red paprika and the *peperoni*, are all part of the same family, but beware of blowing your head off with them.

The greater part of Hungary's paprika harvest goes into producing powder for cooking purposes and there are several small towns and villages across the flat countryside where the air for miles around is pungent from the local factory. In almost any village, too, you can see the fruit strung up on wire or string beneath the eaves of roadside cottages, drying in the sun until it is completely brittle and ready for pounding. The tomato – or *Paradeisen* –

166

paprika makes the sweetest powder, while the reds and yellows are hotter. The degree of 'heat' in the powder is controlled by inclusion of more or less of the dried seeds.

Every district of Hungary, and every district where the Hungarians once ruled or shared rule, has its own variety and, as with many other foods, every district believes its own version is exclusive to itself. The French will tell you that *ratatouille* can be found only in Provence: nonsense – its Magyar name is *lecso*, its Serbian, *djuvec*, and there are at least half-a-dozen other names with only slight modifications in the dish itself. Wherever sheep or goat cheese is eaten, the local people are convinced that only they eat it. The Turkish dish of *moussaka* is to be found far to the north and west of the furthest limits of the Turkish conquests and will always be offered, with a great flourish, as a purely local speciality. Incidentally, continuing the process of mutation, *Larousse Gastronomique* gets the basic goulash recipe wrong. The meat should NOT be browned before cooking: that dish is called *pörkölt*, which means 'singed'.

My own favourite goulash, which is pretty basic, is made like this: take the same quantity of meat and of large white onions – the kind that cook to a pulp. The meat may be pork or beef, preferably half-and-half. In either pork dripping or sunflower-seed oil (goose fat would be an alternative in Hungary) the coarsely chopped onions are stewed in a covered pot until they reduce to a soft mess. On no account may they be fried. If the onions have not absorbed all the fat, add enough flour to soak it up, or alternatively allow the goulash to get cold after cooking and then skim off the top oil. There is a standing argument as to how much onion, and whether flour at all should be used. This is because in Hungary flour is not used for sauces as a rule, and onions and garlic are not considered 'fine' among the classless society of present-day Central and Eastern Europe. However, goulash is not elegant cooking, it is peasants' and workers' food, so that the snobberies of the middle classes have no real place in its preparation. The meat, cut in gobbets of a size to be managed as one forkful, is added to the onion pulp, with salt, thyme, tomato paste or skinned tomatoes and powdered paprika. Don't be afraid of the paprika. Only experience can tell you how much of which variety to use, but for two pounds of meat a tablespoon of sweet paprika and a teaspoon of hot is not too much. Mix all together and it will take on a handsome rich hue. Just cover with water and let it cook up gently and go on cooking while you go about your business for a couple of hours. Remember

167

that fresh tomatoes and pork both make juice rather than dry it up, and need less water. The mixture should simmer for at least two hours, so you need a thick pot with a bottom that does not 'catch'.

Being a lazy cook, I usually then cook non-floury potatoes in their jackets and skin them when cool enough to handle. They go into the pot with the goulash: before taking it off the fire, I throw in a handful of marjoram, which should never be cooked but only left in the heat long enough for the flavour to penetrate. Serve in the pot with dark bread and a roughish red wine. A smoked coarse sausage may be added to the cooked potatoes for the last quarter of an hour to give a smoky taste. A frequent variant of this dish, a *Szekely-gulyas*, is the addition of sauerkraut, which is cooked for about half an hour in the goulash, and of caraway (*Kümmel*) seeds. The sauerkraut should be washed first like any other vegetable and tasted for saltiness, so be mean with the salt when starting the cooking. The flavour of goulash is improved if it is prepared the day before eating and then heated up. Remember, too, that there must be water in anything allowed to cook for hours, but only sufficient water actually to cover the solid food on a slow simmer. Too much water weakens the goulash but excess juice can be kept for the next day's soup. The basic recipe is generally known in Hungary as a *Szegediner*-goulash and there are innumerable permutations in different areas. In Debrecin, the 'capital' of the Puszta, they throw in chunks of the local tough but piquant sausage. In the Balaton Lake region they produce a succulent dish which, for the benefit of foreigners, they term 'fish goulash' but is nothing more complicated than a sort of *bouillabaisse* with paprika added.

Chicken, veal and even lamb are used in some of the more sophisticated Budapest restaurants, but these – like the similar dishes concocted in Vienna – are not properly goulash, since these meats disintegrate if cooked so long. They should be cooked for about half an hour with less liquid, and fresh sliced paprika (peppers) can be used: they are really chicken or veal paprika. In Hungary they often serve a form of pasta with any of these dishes, usually a kind of crumbled egg-and-flour paste called *tarhonya*. The first contact most tourists have with this national Hungarian dish is normally in Vienna, though it is not native to this city, merely imported by historical association with Budapest. The best version in Austria can be found in almost any primitive Vienna pub – more genuine than anything served in more expensive restaurants.

170

If the notion that goulash belongs to *cuisines raffinées*, whether high or household, is a legend, this should not be taken to mean it is anything but excellent food. It was, in fact, an Hungarian who once made to me the limpid statement of only apparent obviousness that any dish tastes of what you put into it. If you use substitute ingredients the food will taste artificial and will provide only inferior nourishment. The Magyars have never manufactured much *ersatz* food, and their rich land provides plenty of simple and tasty things to eat and drink, all efforts of a centrally controlled economy being thwarted by the renowned cantankerousness of the ordinary people. They love to eat and drink, and retain high standards of hospitality, so that a Magyar woman who cannot cook is a rarity. Their foods and wines are rich in vitamins, notably the paprika and tomato pastes they put up in glass for the winter, and various vegetable and fruit pulps. There is no doubt these foodstuffs are not only a pleasure to eat for those who prefer spicy foods, but that they also account for the high level of health and looks among Hungarians, quite apart from extravagant claims of aphrodisiac properties.

I have even heard it argued – by Magyars of course – that the extraordinary incidence of intelligence and talent among Hungarians is a product of their diet; it is much more probable that brain-power comes from struggling in childhood with the fearsome Magyar language and the necessity its exclusiveness imposes, on everyone above the peasant level, to learn at least one other. This need today is much less than it was up to World War II, and it would be an interesting subject for research to discover whether the closed borders of modern Hungary are reducing the standards of intelligence.

Paprika is a preservative in exactly the same way as our tropical pepper: that is, it will not keep meat and fish for ever, but will preserve it longer than it would normally keep. *Lecso* is made with oil and paprika to keep through the winter, purée of vegetables is bottled and preserved, tomatoes and paprika preserved in oil for use in salads, all after the same manner in which we preserve fruits in glass. And, being a preservative, paprika is much used with smoked and dried foods; as a snack to go with the pre-dinner glass of spirits, for instance, Hungarians score into squares a piece of pork-skin and roast it until it is crisped right through and rolls itself up into a cylinder. This is then dusted with sweet paprika and eaten with a fork or broken off in bits with the fingers. Messy, but delicious. It goes marvellously well in winter with the various

171

fruit-brandies of the middle and south-east of Europe – slivovitz, tuiça, barack, as well as vodka or the various types of grain schnapps.

The Hungarians, of course, are, and firmly insist that they are, a 'different' race. The remnants, themselves, of an early nomadic migration from Central Asia, they find themselves today surrounded by Slav tribes and an equally alien Latin strain of Rumanians. Only the Hungarians, and the people in places where Hungarians have taken it, make goulash. To the south and east, in what is loosely called the Balkans, the practice of grazing cattle for the whole summer on wide plains also exists. But the Yugoslav and the Bulgarian herdsmen, living through a hotter summer, tend to rely on lamb and mutton, either as *djuvec*, which contains a lot of paprika, or roasted deliciously over a charcoal fire. A Hungarian goulash would not be suited to their hotter climates and they live very much on ripe sheep's cheese, with bread and raw fruits.

As the custom of holidaying abroad spread in the nineteenth century, so did foreign dishes become naturalised, but the unfamiliarity of the paprika kind of pepper produced changes, so that if one is offered a dish named 'goulash' today in Switzerland or West Germany it will be a thick dark-brown stew with only a pinch of paprika, if there is any at all. An enterprising but desperate Hungarian restaurateur in the Rhineland who set out to tickle the German palate once told me he had given up the struggle after being steadily forced to reduce the degree of spiciness to vanishing point.

All the same, goulash found its way into German army slang. A field kitchen became *Gulasch-kanone*, which needs no translation. The contents are more likely to be a thick soup of dried peas or beans with bacon than goulash, but the word remains. Perhaps Prussian troops adopted the foreign word after the battle of Königgrätz, when they fought the multi-national armies of the Habsburgs. Or it may have been as late as World War I, when Austrian and German armies fought for years side-by-side against the Russians on the vast eastern fronts. Even the civilian spread of cooking goulash may, just possibly, have its origin in military custom. For thousands of Magyar soldiers were stationed in northern Italy during the whole period of the *Risorgimento* and their 'Gulasch-kanonen' certainly contained the real thing. Since Italy, then as now, was a favourite goal of travellers for pleasure, the name and the dish itself may well have spread from Italian cooks who worked for Austro-Hungarian officers to their *cartes de jour* when they worked for hoteliers.

As to goulash itself, change has been for the worse. In Western Europe, professional cooks adhere mainly to the French tradition, and usually therefore (except for the basic soups) seal or singe meats before they are cooked in water or in wine. But if the meat with the paprika is browned before water is added to the goulash, then the paprika loses its pungent flavour and colour and the result is no longer goulash. Contact with non-liquid heat 'kills' the paprika, and the fundamental rule for goulash as for all paprika foods is not to cook paprika dry. On dry foods, such as grilled meat or fish, it is added at the last moment.

As the food itself is simple, so the drinks that go with it. A glass of *eau-de-vie* – one of the typical Central European fruit brandies – may be drunk before the meal, for the goulash will absorb a good deal of alcohol. With the meal, beer is not an anomaly, but as with all other cuisine, the *boisson du pays* goes best with the *plat du pays* and a commonplace, heavy rough red wine is ideal. A fine wine is wasted on goulash, for its taste is drowned in the overpowering flavour of paprika and herbs. The ideal course to follow is a thin pancake filled with apricot pulp, but the plain English cheeses and the hard fruits that go with them, an apple or a pear to be eaten with the cheese, are excellent and entirely in keeping with the simple nature of goulash.

There is at least one shop in Vienna which retains, mysteriously, the provisional character of a street-corner stall in South-eastern Europe, at which one can buy the various qualities and strengths of paprika and other ingredients of goulash. (Paprika Hatschek, Vienna 4, Pressgasse 23.) The shopman is a *devoté* and if you go in there to buy a 'deka' (Viennese for 100 grams) of sweet or sharp paprika, you will be lucky to get out without buying five different kinds, a string of dried peppers and a bottle of Barack.

More usually, paprika sellers are expansive old market-women who sit – sometimes even squat on their haunches – at street corners in every Central and South East European village and town with an old pair of brass scales weighing out paprika, caraway, thyme and bay leaves with a spoon into little triangular paper bags. Most of these itinerant street sellers are either gypsies or Jews. Besides selling their wares, they are, of course, the purveyors of local gossip and equally useful both to the police and to those whom the police seek.

In Budapest, nowadays, the serving of goulash has become a

ritual as a tourist attraction. So, at *Matyas Pince* in Pest, or the *Fortuna* in Buda on the hill, you may watch American ladies of exquisite mien being exaggeratedly warned of the strength of 'our famous national dish', served in miniature cauldrons over spirit flames. The official guide will choke artistically over the first mouthful to prove his point, and will repeat the Hungarian belief that a diet of paprika-flavoured food will arouse the most stubbornly flagging interest in the arts of the bedroom as well as those of the kitchen.

JOHN RUSSELL

On the Bottle

The wine-buyer for Fortnum & Mason writes about a 'byway of antiques' where values have soared in recent years

RACKING DOWN AND acquiring old wine bottles can be as fascinating as any other branch of the collecting game. These specimens are in the collection of Mr Luis Gordon, Senior, now suitably housed in the boardroom of Luis Gordon & Sons, the sherry shippers.

'Sealed bottles', as they are called – seals, bearing the owner's name or crest and sometimes the date, were fused on the bottle at the time it was made – first came into use in England about the middle of the seventeenth century, the art of glass bottle making having been lost since the end of the Roman occupation (2). The earliest specimens have especially tall necks and heavily rounded bodies (3), and since comparatively few have survived they are now rare collectors' items that have rapidly increased in value. Bottles that ten years ago could be had for as little as £10 have fetched £200 in recent sales.

In the second period of design (1660–1700) the bottle is shorter and more of a decanter shape (1, 4–7). These bottles performed two functions – bringing the wine from the cask and as decanters or serving-bottles at the table.

In the third period (1700–1750; 8–11) there was little change in design but refinements in the materials can be observed.

From about 1750 onwards the wine-bottle industry began to be commercialised and at the same time the shape of the bottle was more or less settled as we know it today (12, 13). These bottles were more easily stored (on their sides) while the wine matured. With the introduction of the corkscrew, the cork also took on the more practical role of keeping the bottle airtight. Formerly bottles stood upright and corks, intended to keep out dirt and dust, were tied down and the string attached to the string rim on the neck; this feature persisted, although it no longer had a precise function.

The last period in the history of bottle making is that of mould-blown bottles (14).

Where can the would-be collector of bottles find them today? In street markets, junk shops and of course antique shops. They can turn up in unexpected places; some have been found embedded in walls when derelict sites in cities are being excavated and there are probably many left in unexplored cellars in old properties in the country – the west of England is generally reckoned to be rich territory.

There is not a vast literature on the subject but there are occasionally useful articles in magazines such as *Apollo, Connoisseur* and *Country Life*. A book published in 1949, *Sealed Bottles* by Shealah Ruggles-Brise, is a valuable guide, but it has itself become a collector's item.

(1)   (2)   (3)

(4)   (5)   (6)   (7)

(8) (9) (10) (11)

(12)   (13)   (14)

ELIZABETH RAY

Only One Sauce?

NCE UPON A TIME,
and not for very long, I had a
housekeeper whom I remember mainly because of her excessive
refinement, and the fact that whenever she went out of doors, even
to the dustbin, she put on a fur coat. I think she feared that if it
wasn't firmly anchored to her it would take off for the dustbin
itself. Our dislike was mutual, but our relationship foundered
early and for good on the day she looked into the store cupboard.
'Where,' she asked suspiciously, 'is the O.K.?' I had to confess that
I hadn't any, whereupon she gave notice. Which was O.K. by me.

The Prince Caraccioli, a busy traveller who visited England in
the eighteenth century, is now remembered only for his remark
about England's being a country of sixty religions and only one
sauce. But in fact he was wrong, for even then many of the sauces
that we now know so well were already on the market.

But his idea of a sauce – and this is the classic conception – was
that it is an integral part of the dish, whereas in Britain it is far
more an accompaniment; although certain sauces go traditionally
with certain meats they are not an essential ingredient. Think of the
homely sauces of this country – apple sauce, onion sauce, bread
sauce, horseradish, mint or caper; they are side dishes and do not
denote a particular method of cooking in the same way as, for
example, the name of a *Sole Dugléré*, or *Ris de Veau Financière*,
both of which convey a definite meaning to any chef. They are
'relishes', rather than sauces in the French sense.

Dignified labels of the early nineteenth century.
Johnson's label shows York House, Bath, now the
Royal York Hotel.

Another difference in the English idea of sauces as compared
with the French is that although we are a rich country, with
plentiful supplies of dairy products, our sauces are largely based on
vinegar, not on butter or cream. Most of our sauce culture comes
from India and the Far East, in the same way as so many other
dishes now anglicised, such as curry or kedgeree. Indeed, the names
of chutney and ketchup are Indian or Chinese. Ketchup,
also known as catsup, is said to come from the Chinese *Koe-chiap*
or *Ke-tsiap*, meaning the brine of pickled fish, though it seems to
have originally been used to describe a sauce made from mushrooms, and most likely introduced by employees of the East India
Company. Many people who lived and traded in India became used
to spicy, highly seasoned food, and on their return home brought the

182

 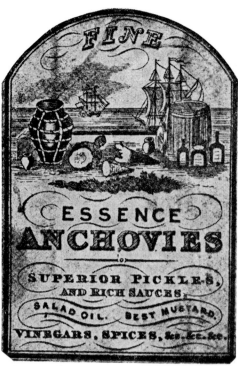

tradition with them. It was also considered smart to have friends
or connections in the East, and it showed sophistication to produce
such things.

Most of these sauces started in the domestic kitchen, but became
more widespread with the beginnings of mass-production at the
time of the Industrial Revolution. The earliest sauces with definite
names and characteristics were called after their originators,
notably Quin's (named after James Quin, an actor and a rival of
Garrick) and Harvey's. These were first produced in a small way,
but with increasing popularity became commercial and sold on
what was for those days a large scale. Their importance is shown
in the sauce labels used at the turn of the eighteenth and nineteenth
centuries. Similar to the silver wine labels that are still familiar,

these little labels were used on the silver and cut-glass cruets of the time, and bore names some of which are still with us, and many that are not. Indian Soy; Camp; Mogul; Walnut Catsup; Carrache; to name only a few. Cab Shelter Sauce is one that is unlikely to have found its way on to any silver label, but this basic sauce was made in many parts of London and served in the shelters where cabbies had their meals. Similar sauces are probably served now to taxi-drivers, but they will be standard products. Each 'cab-crib' had its own version, but basically it was the same – and must have been similar to many of the mass-produced brands – a quantity of shallots, garlic, pepper and mushroom ketchup boiled up with sharp vinegar. 'Burgess's Fish Sauce' had a silver label to itself, and this is a brand that is still well known. The firm of John Burgess was founded as long ago as 1760, when the original Burgess was sent by his father, a country grocer, to start a business in the Strand as 'Oilman and Italian Warehouseman', importing and selling many goods from abroad. In an advertisement in *The Times* in 1788 he announces that he can supply, among other commodities, 'New-foundland Cod's Sound, Rein Deer Tounges [*sic*]; Bologna Sau-sages, with or without garlic; Superfine Sallard Oil; very curious French Olives; Zoobditty Mutch, with a great variety of rich Sauces for Fish, Beefsteaks &c. N.B. Hambro' [*sic*] Sour Croat in any quantity'. Zoobditty Mutch was another Eastern concoction used as a sauce for fish, as the name derives from two Indian words *Joobitty-Matchli* meaning 'tasty' and 'fish'. This particular firm flourishes now as it did when it supplied goods to such famous characters as Nelson, was mentioned by Sir Walter Scott and Byron and, more recently, helped to stock the galley of Captain Scott's ship on his Antarctic expedition.

The main type of sauce marketed then was the thin, dark, pungent Worcestershire variety. The thicker fruity sauces came later. An early example was Yorkshire Relish Thin, which first reached the market in 1837, derived from a private recipe, as were most of these sauces. The words Yorkshire Relish appear in the Yorkshire Archaeological Pipe Roll for Richard II in the latter half of the fourteenth century, and it would be interesting to know exactly what this was. This particular sauce was the subject of a

---

The King of Oude's Favourite Sauce (left) was introduced in 1825; the name of the bottler, Hickson, is moulded in the glass.
The present-day bottle for Burgess's Essence of Anchovies still retains its period flavour.

court case in the last century because so many pirated versions were appearing on the market. Eventually, the House of Lords ruled that the words 'Yorkshire Relish' indicated that the product was that of Goodall, Backhouse & Co, and of no one else, and they still have exclusive rights to the name. It is possibly the only registered sauce name to include a place name: the best-known Worcester sauce may be Lea and Perrins', but the firm does not have an exclusive right to 'Worcester' or 'Worcestershire'.

Harvey's Sauce, also of the thin dark kind, was being widely sold by the middle of the eighteenth century. The story goes that Peter Harvey, who ran a coaching house called *The Black Dog* at Bedfont in Middlesex, concocted an excellent sauce which made him and his inn famous for many miles around. A young grocer called Lazenby became very interested in this wonderful sauce, which he heard Londoners talk about 'with bated breath and shining eyes', and tried hard to buy the recipe, but without success. However, he eventually married Elizabeth Harvey, Peter's sister, to receive the treasured recipe as a wedding present. They put it to good use, and Elizabeth Lazenby and Son became a flourishing business, one that is still known today, although the firm is now absorbed into the Crosse and Blackwell empire.

The original Worcestershire Sauce recipe also came to this country from India, brought over by Sir Marcus Sandys, Governor of Bengal, a century and a half ago. He took the recipe to Mr Lea and Mr Perrins, chemists, with a pharmacy in Broad Street, Worcester. They made the sauce for the governor for some time, but it became so well known and well liked that they eventually obtained the recipe and sold the sauce under their own name, with such success that in 1896 they had to move from their little shop to the factory where the sauce is still made.

The O.K. Fruity Brown Sauce so much liked by my fur-coated housekeeper was first made in 1881, and started very much as a one-man business. George Mason, the originator, used to make the sauce in the morning, then trundle a hand-cart along the King's Road, Chelsea, in the afternoon, selling his product. He did very well and expanded into a private limited company until in the 1890s he ran into financial difficulties and was bought out by a larger company, now part of Colman's.

The container (opposite) in which Soyer's Relish was sold, *c.* 1870. His portrait appeared on most of his jars and pots.

That flamboyant character Alexis Soyer is probably most widely known as the originator of Mutton Cutlets Reform. But he was also much to the fore in the Crimean War, when his ideas and patent cooking apparatus were used to feed the troops at the front. Later, they were used to try to alleviate the sufferings of the Irish during the famine years, when Soyer's soup, while not particularly appetising, was at least nourishing. He also produced a Relish 'which was adapted for all kinds of viands', and by 1848 had produced Soyer's Sauces (*One expressly for the Ladies and the other for the Gentlemen*) – 'a slight shake before pulling the cork is an improvement' – which was sold at 2*s* 6*d* the half pint by Crosse and Blackwell. *Punch* greeted this 'ornament to the table' thus: 'A NEW DEVOURING ELEMENT. You all know Soyer the Philanthropist, who pretends to be so full of his fellow-creatures? Can you doubt it after the following. Read it, and feel "like goose's flesh" all over! – "Soyer's New Sauce for Ladies and Gentlemen!!!" Was there ever such a cannibal? Why, it is regularly settling man against wife, son against mother-in-law, pauper against beadle, boots against cook! No lady, no gentleman is safe. The aristocracy is on the verge of the sauce-boat. We denounce Soyer as the greatest *traiteur* in England, or even Ireland, and the latter is saying, at present, an immense deal.' This last reference is, of course, to his soup-kitchens.

Many of the firms that flourished during the last century or so have disappeared or been absorbed, but Crosse and Blackwell, one of the biggest and best known, had its origins as far back as 1706 and still survives. In that year Messrs West and Wyatt started trading in Shaftesbury Avenue as Oilmen, importing and selling many pickles, relishes and condiments. In 1819 two fifteen-year-old boys were apprenticed to the firm – Edmund Crosse and Thomas Blackwell – who did so well that in 1829, when the Mr Wyatt of the day was due to retire, they prevailed upon their respective families to raise the sum of £600, with which they bought the business.

H.P. Sauce – another household name – also had its origins in the nineteenth century. The Midland Vinegar Company had a small factory near Birmingham, and the owner was given the recipe by a friend. For some years he did not use it very much but eventually put it on the market, with the success we know. Nobody seems to be sure of the significance of the initials; one thought is that it stands for Houses of Parliament, as they appear on the label, and from its earliest days the sauce was used in the refectory there, but I prefer to think of them as the initials of the unknown originator, and the Houses of Parliament as coincidental. It still has a strong Parliamentary connection, as many jokes and references have been made to Mr Wilson's fondness for this particular sauce. But it also has a Royal Appointment: what's good enough for Mr Wilson is good enough for the Queen.

These are all English firms and sauces the best known of them all, Heinz of the 57, does not really belong here, as it has always been an American firm, although most of the sauces with which it made its reputation had their origin here, and it was Mr Heinz who got the licence to make and sell Worcester Sauce in the States.

All these fruity sauces owe much to the Indian chutney, and are all basically the same: a variety of fruits, such as tomatoes, apples, dates, raisins, tamarinds – many, no doubt, now imported in pulp form – cooked and blended with strong vinegar, spices and seasonings. The proportions and blending are closely guarded secrets of each manufacturer. Until now, the regulations only made it necessary to state the ingredients of the fruit sauces, and this has been the custom for most manufacturers. New laws coming into force in 1971 will make it a condition that all ingredients should be shown even in the thin brown sauces, but as the secrets lie more in the blending and not so much in the ingredients these new regulations are unlikely to make much difference to the industry. If I had to hazard a guess at the basic ingredients of these sauces I would say that they were based on soy sauce (of Eastern origin) made more pungent with spices, pepper and vinegar, and in one or two cases with anchovies.

By far the most popular sauces now are those based on the tomato, but in the days when this kind of ketchup originated, the tomato, or tomata as it was often spelled, was not used very much. The basis then was more likely to be a mushroom ketchup. The tomato was regarded with a certain amount of suspicion as it was not really known whether to look upon it as a fruit or vegetable, and nineteenth-century cooks did not always think of it as 'wholesome'. Indeed it is not until the middle of the century that the tomato figures with any prominence in cookery books, and then mainly as a cooked vegetable, and only rarely as a salad.

But in all these cookery books there are chapters devoted to Store Sauces. In those days this meant sauces made at home and kept in the store cupboard. Most of the bottled sauces on the market started off in this homely way, and the name can still be applied, except that it now means sauces bought in a store. They all have

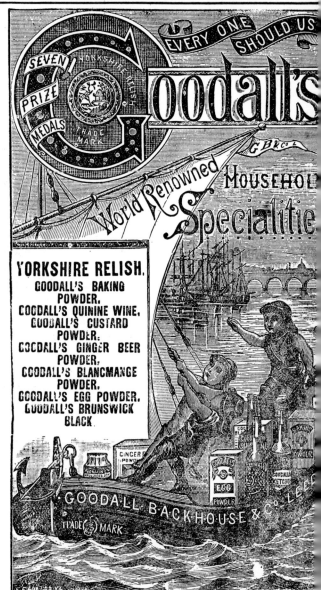

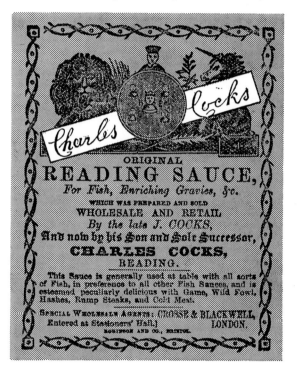

Posters and a press advertisement.
The Nabob advertising is of the 1890s, the press advertisement
opposite being from the *South Eastern Herald,* 1899.
The HP poster is probably from the 1920s or 1930s

192

... **IS A THOROUGHLY COOKED FOOD.**

WHOLESOME, NUTRITIOUS, AND EASILY DIGESTED.

Invaluable for Growing Children, Dyspeptics and Invalids.

RETAILED EVERYWHERE.

Registered Address: "**RIDGE'S FOOD, LONDON.**"

honourable and exotic origins, but the pity is that they have all become the Lazy Cook's Let-Out, too much associated with the dining tables of dreary boarding-houses and second-grade restaurants. An only too familiar sight is the bottle plonked down in the middle of the table with a dribble of dried sauce down its neck, and they are used so freely that every dish tastes alike. But perhaps when one considers some of the food in such places this is not altogether a bad thing.

"He ... he doused it with ketchup."

From *Punch* 24 March 1965

REGINALD PECK

The Longest Wine Lis

ENTURIES AGO,
fearful of dying of thirst
after their deliberations, German town councillors took action that
not only met their own needs, but has remained to the present day
to benefit their heirs, successors and fellow-citizens. In the base-
ments of their *Rathäuser* (Town Halls) they caused to be constructed *Ratskeller* (Councillors' Cellars), where a hearty meal and
appropriate drink could be obtained by all comers. There are many
Ratskeller still scattered about the country, and the modern
traveller can do worse than seek them out.

Among them, the *Rathaus* of the north-German seaport town of
Bremen dates from 1405, and is famous for the length of its wine
list; certainly the longest not only among the *Rathäuser* but in the
entire country – possibly in the world. Any German restaurateur
soon discovers this who is ill-advised enough to claim that his list
of a hundred items or so is the longest. He will get a tart note from
the Bremen *Ratskeller* informing him that *its* list has – well, the
current one starts at the figure 1 and ends at 1500.

It must be admitted at once that the figures are deceptive,
though the cellar authorities do not mean them to be. The facts
are, that the many old wines in the cellar were given their reference
number when they first arrived many years ago and it would be
confusing to all concerned if they were changed. Thus, as the stock
of any given wine is for any reason exhausted and its number not
yet allotted to a newcomer, gaps appear. This may mean consump-

n the World?

tion not only by the normal frequenters of the cellar but by others. During the Napoleonic wars it was once pretty well emptied by the soldiery, and British and Americans who used the cellar after the Second World War as an officers' mess got through the whole of the existing stock except for a few dozen bottles of exceptional age – and probably no longer fit to drink. It amounted in all to the equivalent of some 400,000 bottles, much of which had been in cask. This figure did not include 100,000 bottles stored 'for safety' in the Rheingau nor another 25,000 bottles entirely of Spätlesen, Auslesen, Beerenauslesen, and Trockenbeerenauslesen that were hidden in the Lüneburg Heath. Not a single bottle from either hideout was ever seen again by the cellar authorities, though down whose throats such divine liquids went as those on the Heath no one knows but the owners of the throats themselves.

In spite of all this, the list today is 621 items long, and every one of the *Ratskeller* wines is German, - all the more surprising in that Bremen lies some hundreds of miles from the wine-growing areas of Germany, and is the port through which much French wine now arrives. The reason is that the city authorities, back in Hanseatic days, created a monopoly in Rhine wine (which then included Moselle), obliging dealers to give them priority on all such wines as they had to offer. The local 'authorities' were in the earlier days the local archbishop, whose needs – for the suitable entertainment of local and visiting ecclesiastics – were considerable, and it was his bailiff's job to see that they were met.

Civic authorities in Bremen preserved the tradition, and the wine trade flourished; the *German* wine trade, that is. What it amounted to was that the city authorities of whatever century *profited* from the trade in which they had the exclusive right to buy and sell. So competitors were kept at bay. They crept in only for a brief period in the fifteenth century when some 'southern wines' – Spanish, Portuguese, Italian, and Greek – escaped the notice of the monopoly authorities. Only one of them remains, and that only by name. The *sekt* of today, of which there are a score or so examples on the Bremen list, is a German sparkling wine, while the *seck* or *secq* of the seventeenth century in Bremen was either a Shakespearian style *sack* or some other still, dry, southern *vino seco*.

Lest anyone should suppose that the length of the Bremen list means that there cannot be more than a thimbleful of each wine it should be made clear that the wine casks in the cellar have a capacity of very nearly half-a-million litres and that the number of bottles is rather more than the same figure. But they are not all available to everyone. Some of them are unlisted (generally because great age has turned them into undrinkable museum pieces or because they are wanted for special purposes or occasions). Asterisks in a section of the list marked *Schatzkammer* (Treasure Chamber) mark 140 wines that with two or three exceptions have no price against them. They are offered only at official banquets in the cellar, or to those whom the city wishes to honour.

Like the other former Hanseatic towns, Bremen neither awards orders nor allows its citizens to accept them. When it does desire to show its appreciation of the public services, either of its own citizens or of outsiders, it presents them instead with a gift of fine wine from its famous cellar. The custom arose in the seventeenth century when Frederick the Great was the recipient (several times) of such liquid honours. Although just embarking on the Seven Years' War he found time (1756) to write a personal letter of thanks. Many of Napoleon's marshals received similar awards and so, of course, did the Duke. In more recent times Dr Adenauer, Herr Kiesinger and the new federal president Dr Heinemann have all received wine honours from Bremen.

The treasures in the *Schatzkammer* are all of mouth-watering quality, and include thirty-seven wines from the great year 1953. All but five are marked with an asterisk – for official banquets only – but *without* one is Iphöfer Kammer Silvaner Trockenbeerenauslese (Franken) produced and bottled at the Juliusspital of Würzburg. Price: DM 100 or hardly more than £10. What you cannot buy from the *Schatzkammer* are ten items from the fabulous year 1921 that include a Niersteiner Kehr und Fläschenhahl Riesling Trockenbeerenauslese produced and bottled by Franz Karl Schmitt. The list reaches back to the 1890s with half-a-dozen items and then closes with No. 1500. This is a Rüdesheimer Apostelwein of 1727 and, not being marked with an asterisk, is priced – £5 the half-bottle. They say that if the cost of storage and leakage from cask were allowed for, the price *per glass* would be £4,000. A note says that 1727 was 'according to the records' a quite special year, its wine 'fine, with clearly marked acidity, of great clarity and with a bouquet suggestive of old sherry'.

But if most of the *Schatzkammer* wines are not for him, the normal customer need not think he is being fobbed off with anything. No. 1 on the list, and the cheapest, is a 1968 Westhofener Bergkloster (Rheinhessen) bottled in the *Ratskeller* and priced at DM 4, say 8s 6d. No. 700, the dearest, is a 1959 Avelsbacher Hammerstein Trockenbeerenauslese Fuder 203 (Ruwer) produced and bottled by the Staatliche Domänen-Weinbauverwaltung, Trier, at DM 200 (rather more than £20). Between them are many of the finest hocks and Moselles in the world. There are ten red wines ranging from a 1967 Ober Ingelheimer (Rheinhessen) for DM 5 to a 1959 Assmanshauser Höllenberg Spätburgunder Edelbeerenauslese Cabinet (Rheingau) for DM 100. The *sekt* starts at the cellar's own demi-sec at DM 12 and rises to Schloss Vaux red at DM 30.

The prices quoted here are the *Endpreise* or final prices, meaning that service, the recent and abominable added value tax, the drink tax and (in the case of *sekt*) the sparkling-wine tax are included. But the list also prints the starting price, so that the customer can see just how much extra he is paying. All in all, it amounts to one-third – No. 1, which ends at DM 4, starts at DM 3 and No. 700, which ends at DM 200, starts at DM 150. This may be much, but the double-column presentation is at least fairer than those many lists that show only the starting price, with the extras down below in small print – so that when the final bill comes it has little relation to what the customer thought he was going to be charged, and he feels tricked.

The oldest cask wines in the *Ratskeller* are stored in the Rose Cellar, so jealously guarded that until 1807 it might be entered only in the company of a council official, and for many years after that only with a written permit. The wines there are all known as 'Rose wines' and they include a cask of unlisted Rüdesheimer 1653 and a couple of Moselles from 1723 and 1731. The *Kellermeister* is

Rheinweine

Fortsetzung

Nr.

230 1962er Oppenheimer Herrnberg St.-Nikolaus-Eiswein (Rheinhessen) . . 37,54 50,—
Originalabfüllung Verwaltung der Staatlichen Weinbaudomänen Mainz
reif, feine Fruchtsäure

231 1967er Hattenheimer Nussbrunnen Riesling Cabinet Auslese (Rheingau) . 37,54 50,—
Originalabfüllung Freiherrlich Langwerth von Simmern'sche Kellerei Eltville
edle Art

232 1959er Schloss Eltz
Rauenthaler Gehrn Riesling Auslese (Rheingau) . . . . . . 37,54 50,—
Originalabfüllung Gräflich Eltz'sche Gutsverwaltung Eltville
edle Reife und Frucht

233 1967er Schloss Vollrads Auslese (Rheingau) . . . . 37,54 50,—
Originalabfüllung Weingut Graf Matuschka-Greiffenclau
hochedel

234 1964er Oppenheimer Sackträger Riesling Beerenauslese (Rheinhessen) . 37,54 50,—
Originalabfüllung Weingut Reinhold Senfter, Nierstein
feine Reife und Würze

235 1963er Niersteiner Kehr Riesling — Christwein-Eiswein-Strohwein —
(Rheinhessen) — am 24. 12. 1963 gekeltert — . . . . 37,54 50,—
Originalabfüllung Weingut Winzermeister H. Seip
große Süße

236 1964er Niersteiner Brückchen hochfeine Auslese — Jungfernwein —
(Rheinhessen) . . . . 37,54 50,—
Originalabfüllung Weingut Seebrich   1/1 Fl. 18,76 25,—
feinste Reife und Würze — Preismünze in Gold —

237 1959er Binger Scharlachberg Riesling Auslese (Rheinhessen) . . . . 37,54 50,—
Originalabfüllung Weingut Villa Sachsen
großer Edelwein

238 1962er Niersteiner Glöck Riesling St.-Barbara-Eiswein Edelgewächs
(Rheinhessen) — am 4. 12. 1962 geerntet — . . . . 45,05 60,—
Originalabfüllung Verwaltung der Staatlichen Weinbaudomänen Mainz
reife, pikante Fruchtsäure

239 1966er Schloss Johannisberger Rosalack Allerheiligen-Eiswein Auslese
— Braut des Jahrgangs — (Rheingau) . . . . 45,05 60,—
Originalabfüllung des Fürst von Metternich'schen Domäne
eine Rarität

240 1964er Schloss Vollrads Auslese (Rheingau) . . . . 45,05 60,—
Originalabfüllung Weingut Graf Matuschka-Greiffenclau
feinste Fruchtsüße, Duft und Spiel

241 1959er Schloss Reinhartshauser Cabinet
Erbacher Rheinhell Auslese (Rheingau) . . . . 45,05 60,—
Originalabfüllung Administration des Prinzen Friedrich von Preussen
reif, feine Würze

242 1959er Steinberger Auslese Cabinet (Rheingau) . . . . 45,05 60,—
Originalabfüllung Verwaltung der Staatsweingüter Eltville
edle Reife und Fülle

243 1966er Niersteiner Glöck Riesling Beerenauslese Edelgewächs
Faß-Nr. 674 (Rheinhessen) . . . . 45,05 60,—
Originalabfüllung Verwaltung der Staatlichen Weinbaudomänen Mainz
Reife, Würze und Frucht

244 1964er Dienheimer Paterhof Ruländer und Gewürztraminer
Beerenauslese (Rheinhessen) . . . . 45,05 60,—
Originalabfüllung Weingut Herbert Stampp
große Süße und Wucht

245 1964er Bodenheimer Hoch Riesling und Silvaner Beerenauslese
Edelgewächs (Rheinhessen) . . . . 45,05 60,—
Originalabfüllung Verwaltung der Staatlichen Weinbaudomänen Mainz
Reife, Würze und Harmonie

246 1964er Niersteiner Hipping Riesling hochfeine Auslese
— Strohwein-Heiliger Dreikönigswein — (Rheinhessen)
— am 6. 1. 1965 gekeltert — . . . . 45,05 60,—
Originalabfüllung Weingut Winzermeister H. Seip   1/1 Fl. 22,53 30,—
üppige Süße

Der erstgenannte Preis ist der Nettopreis und der zweite der Endpreis, in letzterem sind Bedienungsgeld,
Getränkesteuer und Mehrwertsteuer enthalten.

Rheinweine

247 1959er *Niersteiner Glöck Riesling Auslese Edelgewächs*
— bestes Faß — VNR 146 (Rheinhessen)   45,05   60,—
Originalabfüllung Verwaltung der Staatlichen Weinbaudomänen Mainz
hochedel

248 1962er *Kreuznacher Krötenpfuhl Riesling Auslese Nikolaus-Eiswein*
Nr. 6254 (Nahe)   56,31   75,—
Originalabfüllung Weingut Paul Anheuser
reif, Fruchtsäure

249 1966er *Schloßböckelheimer Kupfergrube Riesling hochfeiner Eiswein*
Kabinettwein (Nahe)   56,31   75,—
Originalabfüllung Verwaltung der Staatlichen Weinbaudomänen
Niederhausen-Schloßböckelheim
feine Süße und Eleganz

250 1962er *Niersteiner Glöck Riesling St.-Nikolaus-Eiswein*
(Rheinhessen) — am 6. 12. 1962 geerntet —   56,31   75,—
Originalabfüllung Verwaltung der Staatlichen Weinbaudomänen Mainz
reif, feinwürzig

251 1965er *Aßmannshäuser Höllenberg Spätburgunder Rot-Weiß*
Beerenauslese Cabinet Faß-Nr. 33 (Rheingau) . . . . . .   —,—   —,—
Originalabfüllung Verwaltung der Staatsweingüter Eltville
edle Reife und Frucht – Goldene Kammerpreismünze –   ¹/₄ Fl.   28,53   38,—

252 1959er *Schloss Vollrads Auslese (Rheingau)*   56,31   75,—
Originalabfüllung Weingut Graf Matuschka-Greiffenclau
großer Edelwein mit feiner Fruchtsäure   ¹/₄ Fl.   28,53   38,—

253 1964er *Schloss Eltz*
Eltviller Sonnenberg Riesling Beerenauslese (Rheingau)   56,31   75,—
Originalabfüllung Gräflich Eltz'sche Güterverwaltung
große Reife und Fülle

254 1964er *Schloss Schönborn*
Marcobrunner Riesling Beerenauslese (Rheingau)   56,31   75,—
Cabinetabfüllung der Gräflich von Schönborn'schen Kellerei Hattenheim
edle Reife und Würze

255 1959er *Hallgartener Jungfer Riesling Beerenauslese (Rheingau)* . . .   56,31   75,—
Originalabfüllung Vereinigte Weingutsbesitzer
Edelsüße und Frische

256 1964er *Oppenheimer Sackträger Riesling Beerenauslese Edelgewächs*
(Rheinhessen)   60,07   80,—
Originalabfüllung Verwaltung der Staatlichen Weinbaudomänen Mainz
Reife und Feinheit

257 1964er *Hochheimer Domdechaney Riesling Beeren-Auslese Cabinet*
Faß-Nr. BA 2 (Rheingau)   60,07   80,—
Originalabfüllung Domdechant Werner'sches Weingut
hochfeins, edle Art und Körper   ¹/₄ Fl.   30,03   40,—

258 1959er *Schloss Reinhartshausener Cabinet*
Erbacher Herrnberg Beerenauslese (Rheinhessen)   60,07   80,—
Originalabfüllung Administration des Prinzen Friedrich von Preußen
edel, hochfeine Frucht

259 1964er *Wachenheimer Goldbächel Riesling Beerenauslese (Pfalz)* . . .   60,07   80,—
Originalabfüllung Weingut Dr. Bürklin-Wolf
feine Reife, Körper und Harmonie — Silberne Preismünze –

260 1967er *Schloss Vollrads Beerenauslese Faß-Nr. 60/133 (Rheingau)* . . .   75,07   100,—
Originalabfüllung Weingut Graf Matuschka-Greiffenclau
hochedel, feine Frucht und Würze

261 1964er *Schloss Eltz Beerenauslese*
Rauenthaler Baiken Riesling Faß-Nr. 426 (Rheingau)   75,07   100,—
Originalabfüllung Gräflich Eltz'sche Güterverwaltung, Eltville
hochfeine, edle Frucht

262 1959er *Rauenthaler Wülfen Beerenauslese (Rheingau)*   75,07   100,—
Originalabfüllung Winzerverein
große Edelsüße, allerfeinste Würze

263 1959er *Hallgartener Jungfer Riesling Edelbeerenauslese (Rheingau)* . .   75,07   100,—
Originalabfüllung Winzergenossenschaft
ganz großer Edelwein

Der erstgenannte Preis ist der Nettopreis und der zweite der Endpreis, in letzterem sind Bedienungsgeld,
Getränkesteuer und Mehrwertsteuer enthalten.

honest enough to admit that these ancient liquids are 'less for the palate than for the nose' and claims them only as 'a part of German wine history'. The Rose Cellar is illuminated only by candles, in the light of which glows the painted figure of the Rose Virgin herself; the great rose on the ceiling is said to be the work of an Italian artist of long ago who had no other means of paying his bill.

No less honoured than the *Rosekeller* is the *Apostelkeller*, where six great casks bear the names of apostles. Their contents are known as *Apostel* wines and include Rüdesheimer 1748, 1766 and 1784, a Hochheimer of 1727 and a Johannisberg 1783. Just as Diedrich Meyer, a former mayor of Bremen, sang the Rose wines in verse, so Heinrich Heine included the *Apostel* wines in his *Song of the North Sea*.

Other sights and sounds that will interest the modern visitor almost as much as what he eats and drinks are the great and ancient casks in the entrance hall of the *Ratskeller*, the Hauff Room with its legends and the frescoes commemorating them, and the echoes that are to be heard there. The biggest of the casks dates from 1737 and can hold enough wine to fill 37,000 bottles. The oldest of them were made in 1623. They are all carved and painted with masks and flowers, the arms of the town and of local patrician families. But the casks are display pieces, only to be admired. The temperature of the hall where they stand is unsuited to wine storage, and they are empty.

The Hauff Room is so named because the poet Wilhelm Hauff wrote his *Fantasies* there, based on the cellar and its legends. The frescoes show a hard-drinking soldier of the Thirty Years' War who is said by Hauff to have sold his soul, Faust-like, to the devil in exchange for the right to become *Kellermeister* in Bremen – and so to unlimited drink.

The Hauff Room is also famous for its echoes; so much so, that a guide book of 1848 says: 'Dear reader, should you chance to find yourself there in the company of an elderly husband with a young wife take care to place the husband in the middle. Otherwise the thoughts the fine old wines are likely to put into your mind will reach his ears as you whisper them to his wife.'

The *Priölken*, or alcoves leading off from the main rooms, were constructed shortly after 1600 and were intended in the first place for sea-captains talking business with their owners. Stoves were lighted, the doors with which the *Priölken* were provided were shut, and all was splendidly suited – for other activities besides business. But any swain of today who mistakes a *Priölke* for a *salle privée* will find himself thwarted, for by a strictly enforced rule the door must be left open unless three or more people are inside. The word *Priölke* itself is local and of peculiar origin. They say it started with the latin *pratum* – meadow – and is thus the word from which the *Prater* of Vienna and the *Prado* of Madrid derive. But then the Flemish got hold of it and turned it somehow (don't ask me how) into *Priel* or *Priöl* – a small, cosy room.

Among the splendid official occasions when *Schatzkammer* and other fine wines from the *Ratskeller* are drunk the *Schaffermahlzeit* is the most important. It started centuries ago when, after laying up for the winter, the ships of Bremen prepared – in February – to set sail again. The captain and their owners gathered for a final business talk in the local House of the Sea over which elected dignitaries or *Schaffer* (a local word derived from *schaffen* – to achieve) presided. *Mahlzeit* means literally a 'meal' but it is in practice always dinner; still always in February but now in the *Ratskeller*. Distinguished guests are invited but they must not be Bremen folk and must not be invited more than once. The tradition is maintained that long clay pipes should be smoked but the blotting-paper napkins of earlier times have given way to linen. The traditional opening course of dried fish known as *Stockfisch* is still served though not always appreciated (they whisper) by the modern non-Bremen palate. *Stockfisch* is followed by the somewhat startling name *Pinkel* – startling because it is the normal colloquialism for that liquid into which the human system turns even the wines of the Bremen *Ratskeller*. At the *Schaffermahlzeit* it turns out to be a pork dripping and oatmeal *Wurst*, which may be as unpalatable to many as the *Stockfisch*. But both must be eaten by the guests, much as that desert delicacy, sheep's eyes, must be eaten when offered by the sheik. Still, with those wines as an accompaniment . . .

EDMUND PENNING-ROWSELL

Wines to Buy an

THIS CHAPTER IS
addressed particularly to the serious
wine-buyer and drinker, who makes regular provision for the future
by laying down wine either at home or in his wine merchant's
cellar. This requires thought as well as money, but for those who
live more or less from bottle to mouth there is less difficulty in
buying wine in Britain than at any time since the Middle Ages,
when wine was the staple drink in the numerous taverns. For the
advent of the big brewery groups into the wine business has
brought with it a great expansion in the availability of wines; and
this has been helped too by the proliferation of off-licences. In
particular there have been great developments in branded wines,
and although a high proportion of these wines may not be particularly good, or perhaps are badly handled, their cost, often in litres,
is not heavy and choice not difficult.

Yet these 'convenience wines' are not really the best value,
because of the high proportion, in the total cost, of import, bottling
and duty charges as well as of promotion outlay. In *The Compleat
Imbiber* 6 (1963) I pointed out that the in-bin, duty-paid cost to a
wine merchant of a bottle of water if it were imported as wine was
about 5*s*; today the figure must be about 8*s*.

So for quality one must look a little higher: to the basic wines
offered by most wine merchants, sold as Médoc, Mâcon Rouge or
Blanc, Graves Supérieures, Beaujolais *tout court*, or wines from such
Eastern European countries as Bulgaria, Hungary or Yugoslavia.

For such wines, and those from the more modest French *appellation contrôlée* districts such as the Loire, Rhône and Alsace, as
well as from Italy and the lesser German areas, there is no buying

208

Wines to Drink in 1971

problem, and their cost has barely kept pace with inflation. For at the lower levels there is a near – if not actual – surplus of wine in the world today, although in Britain the low cost of these wines, so obvious to the visitor to the countries in which they are grown, is obscured by our high duty rate which in 1970 is 5s 4½d per normal-sized (75 cl.) bottle, for wine imported in cask or container.

It is another matter with what may be called the fine wines. Here, as in most other commodities, inflation is a ruling factor, but vintage wines are also affected by another circumstance: restricted supply but growing demand. Broadly speaking, the vineyards from which such wines come cannot be enlarged. It is true that in certain of the *appellation contrôlée* districts of France some new planting or re-planting of former vineyards has been allowed: in the Médoc where the inter-war slump had reduced acreage; in Champagne where the area under vines has been increasing steadily by about 1500 acres a year; in the Rhône at Châteauneuf-du-Pape, and in the Loire in such popular districts as Sancerre. Moreover, there has been a considerable increase in productivity, owing to reduction in loss by diseases of the vine and by the selection of more productive grape varieties. In Burgundy, for example, output is much higher than it was a couple of generations ago, but in the close-packed terraces of the small German wine districts little expansion has been possible.

Yet in the last decade or so there has been a marked increase in world demand for fine wines, notably for leading Bordeaux châteaux and single-vineyard burgundies, and also for estate-bottled Rhines and Moselles. Some of this rising demand comes from the United States of America, recovered at last from the legacy of the Prohibi-

209

tion era. Contrary to a common view, they are not only interested in the top names, but in those wines such as Beaujolais, Pouilly Fuissé, Châteauneuf-du-Pape and Tavel, which have become familiar through promotion in the U.S.A. A marked factor in pushing up the price of the short-crop Pouilly Fuissé 1969 was American demand.

The easiest way to demonstrate the inflation of wine prices is to look back at the wine lists of the year in which *The Compleat Imbiber* first appeared in book form – 1957. Turning them over, I find Ch. Pétrus 1952 on Avery's list at 19*s* 9*d* a bottle, English-bottled. Today the whole crop of Pétrus is château-bottled, and the price of the 1967, the last year available, is well over £3 a bottle. The 1952, château-bottled, is still on Avery's list at 97*s* 6*d* a bottle. On Harvey's 1957 list one could find Ch. Mouton-Rothschild 1950 at 25*s*, and on the Wine Society's list a Ch. Villemaurine 1929, château-bottled, at 25*s*. Their English-bottled Ch. Talbot 1953 was 10*s*. The 1964 wine of this growth is on the latest Wine Society list at 27*s* 6*d*.

Only a dozen years ago, wine merchants had older wines on their lists. Avery's listed four nineteenth-century clarets, and more than thirty from before the last war; Harveys had a couple of 1937s. Increased interest in old wines, combined with the accountants' demand for quicker turnover, have severely reduced the stock of all old vintage wines.

Moreover, the demand for the big 'names' has increased disproportionately. Already the top French growths, which a dozen years ago were accessible in price to the extent of a few bottles for any serious wine-drinker, are now out of the range not only of most wine amateurs, but of most British wine merchants. For this, wealthy Americans must take the responsibility. Just as a century ago nearly all the first growths found their way into the cellars of the British nobility and gentry, now they are the preserve of those Americans who like to buy what they are told is the best.

Among the top clarets, in the United States the leader is Lafite, in spite of the attractions of the similarly Rothschildian Mouton, and the American ownership of Haut Brion. So it is revealing to record the opening price of Lafite per tonneau, as offered to the Bordeaux merchants, in specimen vintages over the past fifteen years. The franc was devalued by 20% in 1957 and a further 17½% in 1958. In 1960 the New Franc, worth one franc for every hundred Old Francs, was introduced. The 1959 Lafite was offered in 1960 at the new rate, so in order to compare the earlier prices with the later, two noughts must be deducted from the Old Franc prices or two added to the New Francs.

Ch. Lafite	1953	300,000 francs	1964	23,000 francs
	1955	500,000	1966	27,000
	1959	11,000	1967	27,000
	1961	27,000	1968	22,500*

Nineteen-sixty-one was a very short vintage; 1968 a very poor one. To give some idea of the change in British prices, I bought Ch. Lafite 1953 at £1 a bottle in 1956; the opening price for the 1967 is not less than £4.

Leaving these heights, a similar though less inflated story could be recorded of other fine wines, and they show the progress of demand and inflation. Although in earlier issues I have warned readers about the rise in wine prices, if anything I underestimated them. In *Imbiber* 4 (1961) I wrote: 'It may seem unlikely now that, for example, 1955 port will cost £5 or more a bottle in 1980, or that top-ranking 1959 clarets will be selling for £6 or £7 a bottle by the mid-1970s, but present prices would have seemed astronomical twenty years ago.'

Well, the advance in price of vintage ports is relatively slow until they are mature, but by the spring of 1970 at Christie's the prices of the five Bordeaux top growths of the 1959 vintage had reached the following heights:

Ch. Lafite	1900s per dozen
Haut Brion	1500s
Mouton Rothschild	1500s
Latour	1400s
Margaux	1550s

Lafite had already topped the apparently unlikely upper limit in not much above half the suggested period, and Haut Brion and Mouton Rothschild had already passed the lower figure.

Moreover, Lafite 1953, mentioned in the same number as selling at 30s a bottle in 1961, has now fetched at auction as much as 2150s a dozen, just on £9 a bottle.

* *The price of Lafite 1969 had not been announced by the time this went to press, but rumour placed it at well over 50,000 N.F.*

The moral of these figures is plain: to buy the fine wine one likes at prices that one can afford, one must buy early. Even if first growths are no longer in our wine world, some of the same reasons for their steady increase in price affect lesser wines; in terms of current prices vintage wine is likely to become more and more expensive. A contributory factor is the need nowadays for wine merchants to turn over their stock as quickly as possible. So fine wines are offered almost as soon as they are in bottle, and the most popular soon go.

Two further factors should encourage early buying. The acceptance of the French *appellation contrôlée* system in Britain – inevitable if we enter the European Common Market – would certainly increase the price of many French wines, particularly burgundies. This is not the place to discuss this complicated, controversial matter, but the present fact is that a good deal of entirely authentic *A.C.* wine is sold in Britain without the *appellation* certificate, cheaper than it would be with it. This is partly owing to surplus production, partly through the manipulation of the official authenticating paperwork, the *acquit vert*. There is also a good deal of French wine sold inside and outside that country bearing labels that do not accord with the contents of the bottle. This applies to wines with *A.C.* as well as without it. This happens chiefly with burgundy, but also with the wine of other districts, where 'cutting' authentic wines with cheaper blends is profitable. It should not apply, however, to estate-bottled wines from any French source, whatever reservations may be made about some of these products.

The non-application in Britain of the French *A.C.* law means that the authenticity of wine sold here depends on the integrity and skill of importers and merchants. Whether with the adoption of *A.C.* we will then receive superior wines is a matter of argument; on the whole I believe that we shall not. For it must be remembered that the system is designed basically to protect the grower, and only incidentally the consumer. Indifferent wines from disastrous years like 1963, 1965 and 1968 have bravely flaunted their perfectly genuine *acquits verts*.

The other local consideration encouraging early purchase in Britain is the rising level of customs duty. It is hard to believe that after Gladstone in 1860 reduced the duty on table wines to 2d a bottle it stayed unchanged for nearly forty years until in 1899, under the pressure of Boer War expenditure, it was advanced by a further ½d a bottle, an increase which no doubt provoked much

PREVIOUS PAGE: Grapes ripening at Château d'Yquem
ABOVE: St Emilion

FOLLOWING PAGE: The Great Romanée Conti

head-shaking among wine merchants and their customers. But the growers' price of fine wines had scarcely altered in the forty or fifty years before the First World War. Those were the days – but not for the growers.

In part, the rise in wine duties is a reflection of inflation. In 1957, the duty on a bottle of wine imported in cask was 2s 1d. In early 1970 it is 5s 4½d, an increase of 150%. Those who bought a case of 1955 claret in 1957 and paid the duty have saved 39s 6d a dozen in duty alone.

Before discussing the actual purchases in 1971, two questions need answering. The first is, how much wine do you drink in a year?

An annual stock-taking carried out in conjunction with a file of the year's wine invoices and a note of any presents is one way of establishing annual consumption; but a more sensible and easy method is to keep a cellar book, of which several examples are now on the market. Indeed I often wonder how any serious-minded drinker can be without one. Not only does this conveniently, compactly contain the business side of wine-drinking; the quantity, date of acquisition and the cost of a wine. It also records development as each bottle is drunk, and the people one drinks it with.

The next question is: how much wine do you own, in your cellar or merchants' reserves? For example, with relatively generous quantities of 1966 burgundies on call, the less consistent 1967s and even the expensive 1969s might be bought scantily, and the former omitted altogether. Unlike wine merchants of standing, we are not called on to represent every respectable vintage in our cellars. I bought no 1957 clarets and very little 1962 red burgundy. For the former I did not care, and had enough of rather older wines not to have to depend much on the latter. On the other hand, having invested rather heavily in 1959 clarets, I almost skipped the 1960s; and this was a mistake.

Few of us have enough money or room to buy all the wines that catch our fancy, and the more we can organise our purchasing the better. There are those who fear to buy too much wine, or to pass away with a cellarful, but heirs and friends are more likely to bless your name if they are left a few bottles to do it in.

One of the most difficult decisions to make is how much of a wine to acquire; particularly if, as recommended, wine is bought when very young, and its prospects must often be left to expert advisers. If argument still continues over the future of the quarter-century old 1945 clarets, and few are certain how the 1964 red burgundies will finally show, it is not surprising that even the most skilled wine merchants cannot be too sure how two- and three-year-old red wines will mature.

By and large, I believe that the minimum requirement for vintage red wine in the 15s to 30s bracket is one dozen bottles. This provides the possibility of sampling a wine over the years, long after it will have been exhausted in a merchant's list. To have enough of a good wine for it to be sampled twelve times over a long period is a modest target to aim at.

A predominantly burgundy-drinker may wish fairly to represent claret in his cellar, but not at the expense of his favourite wine. Many people like to have Rhône wines, but may not wish to acquire a dozen bottles of any one wine – though wines like Hermitage and Châteauneuf-du-Pape, strong and even coarse at first, certainly repay keeping.

For white wines, including German wines, half a dozen is probably a fair initial order, for the bottles can be opened much earlier than with young red wines, and so may probably be replaced before running out of stock.

Marginal interest or high price may reduce the purchases of a young claret or red burgundy. Half-dozens of the amiable light Givry from the Côte Chalonnaise or inexpensive Côtes de Bourg; agreeable wines for everyday drinking or as introductions to more distinguished wines. Beaujolais, another early maturing wine, may be picked up in small quantities; if one vintage is a failure the odds are that the next one will return to drinkable form.

In reply to the question often asked these days as to whether the first-growth clarets, which in this context must include Ch. Mouton Rothschild, Ch. Cheval Blanc and Ch. Pétrus, are worth their prices in relation to other leading clarets, the answer is almost certainly no. For their high price owes something to speculation. In my view Ch. Palmer is often superior to its neighbour, Ch. Margaux – although never so good as the latter at its best. Ch. La Mission Haut Brion can challenge its rival Ch. Haut Brion across the road. If Ch. Lafite may turn out the finest Médoc of the year, and Ch. Mouton Rothschild the most distinctive, neither wine is always the success its price implies; and, across the rivers, I have found Vieux Château Certan almost the peer of Ch. Pétrus – and in 1955, at least, the better wine.

This said, it cannot be denied that these great wines possess unrivalled interest, and not just for wine-snobbery reasons. For in fine years they do set a standard, even if individually they themselves may not always live up to it. Accordingly, it is worth making some room in one's budget and cellar for a few of these rarities, and then back them up with representatives of the second rank.

With top-level burgundies the question is much more difficult, owing to the great variation in the way that the wines are made – to say nothing of the 'stretching' practised with great names in short supply. After all, in a good year there are only about 100 casks of Richebourg for the whole world, but the label is not so rare as the statistics suggest. For me, some very fashionable growers' red burgundies are too sweet and too soft, lacking in body. Two burgundies from the same vineyard may be so different as to denote a different source, although both may be quite authentic.

Nevertheless, in a good burgundy cellar it is desirable to represent the leading names, such as Chambertin, Clos de Vougeot, Richebourg and Musigny; but the type of wine chosen must depend on personal preference. Indeed, the hazards of selecting burgundy can only be overcome with the assistance of those few merchants who buy their burgundies as carefully as they do their Bordeaux; but the difficulties may be reduced by going for the second-rank single-vineyard wines, such as Mazis Chambertin, Vosne Malconsorts, Chambolle Charmes, Beaune Grèves and Volnay Santenots. These wines, less sought after than the top names, may be more authentic than these or such commune wines labelled as Gevrey-Chambertin or Pommard.

This also applies to the white burgundies. Better a good Bâtard Montrachet than a somewhat doubtful Montrachet; and although there are excellent wines labelled plain Meursault, there are an awful lot of bad ones too. A single-vineyard wine like Meursault Charmes is preferable, and Puligny Combettes more reliable than simple Puligny-Montrachet.

In Germany vineyard names abound so greatly – although the new German Wine Law will prune the number substantially in mid-1971 – that most wine-buyers are more hindered than helped by their proliferation, however genuine. The result in Britain is a very small demand for German wines other than for the brands, particularly Liebfraumilch, which may be considered the mother of all branded wines. Designed largely for the restaurant trade, these tend to be expensive for what they are. The most reliable German wines are those produced by certain institutions and large growers, many of them merchants as well.

The reliable institutions include the State Domaines of the Moselle, Rheingau and Franconia, the religious and secular corporations such as the Bischöfliches Konvikt and Friedrich-Wilhelm Gymnasium of Trier, the Juliusspital and Burgerspital of Würzburg, and the various co-operatives or Winzervereins, which can produce excellent wine in their localities.

Among the German grower-merchants are Bürklin-Wolf and Basserman-Jordon of the Pfalz, Schönborn, Von Zimmern and Wegeler of the Rheingau, Ott of Franconia, Kesselstatt of Trier, Gessert of the Rheinhesse, Plettenberg and Anheuser of the Nahe. These concerns usually own a number of scattered vineyards, but there are also a few well-known growers, whose properties are more or less concentrated. These include von Schubert at Maximin Grünhaus, J. J. Prüm at Wehlen and Werner in Hochheim.

The only other vintage wine that calls for early laying down is port. Specific vintages are mentioned below, but a word here about the shippers' names is worth while. It need hardly be said that no wine in the past has been more subject to snobbery than vintage port. Yet it is only about a hundred years since the Oporto shippers first affixed their names to the ports they sold; previously they were sold under the name of the importing merchant who bought and bottled them.

Since then, fashions in the popularity of one shipper or another have varied; and it may be doubted whether this has been of much benefit to the port trade, for some excellent shippers have gone under or been merged because they did not bear the super-fashionable names of the time. Today the top name is certainly Taylor, followed by Cockburn and Graham, and then – in alphabetical order lest unconsciously I seem to imply a hierarchy – Croft, Dow, Fonseca, Sandeman and Warre. Until about forty years ago nearly all the leading names were British, but da Silva's Quinta do Noval broke through with its astonishingly big, fruity 1931. So Noval is almost in the top rank of popularity. Another Portuguese house to make excellent vintage wine is Calem. Owing to our high duty on fortified wines (currently $9s\ 0\frac{1}{2}d$ a bottle), the difference in opening prices between the leading and the lesser names is not very great; a matter of two or three shillings at most. Anybody buying vintage port as an investment is advised to stick to the fashionable names, for it is these that count in the sale room; otherwise a wine merchant may be able to advise on less expensive brands.

Before discussing varieties and vintages of wines we might purchase in 1971, it is worth remembering a factor inevitably unknown as this chapter is written: the quantity and quality of the

220

1970 vintage. However modest our acquisitions of any vintage, it is as well to consider the year before and its successor; and in 1971 the 1969s will be just coming into view. Now, the outstanding fact about the 1969 vintage in Western Europe was its paucity, followed inescapably by prices enhanced by the earlier failure of the 1968s. In Germany, too, the revaluation of the mark added 10% to the export price of all German wines.

There is no doubt that some very fine burgundies were made in 1969; and the smallness of the crop was a factor in its high quality. Following the late vintage there was an immediate dash to buy the young wine while available. The trend was set in the Hospices de Beaune's sale of its own wine in November 1969. The highest price was given for the white Corton Charlemagne François de Salins, which made 13,000 francs a cask (nearly £1000); at the previous sale in 1967 the same *cuvée* fetched 5500 francs.

So whether or not during 1971 we actually buy any 1969 burgundies – and the whites will be the first on offer – we shall certainly have to take account of them sooner or later. For although the 1970s may well be less expensive, it is very rare indeed in Burgundy to have two really fine years in succession.

For Bordeaux the situation is more complicated, since the 1969s appear not to be of outstanding quality, the prices are high, and we have other vintages to fall back on. Here we can afford to wait until the results of 1970 are clear; in any case the 1969 clarets will not generally be on offer in Britain until 1972. Time is on our side.

In both these areas we can spend most of our 1970 budget on topping up the bins of older vintages, particularly the 1966s, which we should have started acquiring in 1969 and 1970. They are fruity wines, but probably fairly quick maturers. In each case they are superior to the 1967s, except in Beaujolais where the later vintage was very fine and may still be worth buying in 1971. The 1967 Côte d'Or wines were rather written-down owing to unevenness and a very small crop. The total *A.C. récolte* was only 175,000 hl. compared with 265,000 hl. in 1966. Nevertheless, some sound 1967s were made, and are certainly worth considering both for reds and whites, particularly by those building up their reserves. However, these wines will not be cheap, whereas the plentiful 1967 clarets are: they are estimated to be light, quick-maturing wines, and they may fulfil a function similar to the amiable, not over-exciting 1962s.

While merchants' stocks last at reasonable prices, the 1964

clarets and burgundies are still worth buying, though remembering the disparity in success among 1964 clarets. This vintage at six to seven years of age has the obvious advantage of reasonable maturity, and the same applies to the 1962s, which should still be worth investing in for early drinking; they may not improve much, but neither should they deteriorate rapidly. The best year to buy now for white burgundy is 1966, followed by 1967, although certain distinguished French-bottled 1964 wines may still be sound.

Among German wines, where vintages are among the earliest to appear in merchants' lists, and the first to vanish, the 1969s are strong candidates for 1971 purchase. By and large, the vintage was better than any since 1966, and in quality as good as that year and as 1964; but the crop was small, about 70% of normal, and the prices high. Although the results of the 1970 vintage will be known before the end of this year, the prospects of two good years running on the Rhine and Moselle are even less than in Burgundy. The 1967s will still be worth buying next year, and in particular the excellent Franconian wines, where finer wine was made than in 1966.

The only problem for vintage-port drinkers in 1971 is whether they have enough of older vintages, for on present indications the last year to be declared generally was 1966, followed by two or three shippers offering 1967. Moreover, while institutions are wise to buy at opening prices the often considerable quantities of individual vintage ports, it may often pay those with more modest needs to buy older years. For vintage port does not appreciate greatly in price for its first decade, and maturity is worth paying for in a wine that takes so long to come round. So the years to buy now might be 1958, 1960 and 1963.

As the buying and storing of vintage wine is generally a more difficult operation than its opening and consumption, so the question of what wines to drink in 1971 may be dispatched fairly briefly.

We are still fortunate in Britain in maintaining a tradition of keeping wine until it is reasonably mature. This was brought home to me at a banquet at Clos de Vougeot in November 1969 when all the three red burgundies served were of the 1966 vintage; to my taste far from ready.

The red burgundies we may now be drinking will be 1962s, 1964s and 1959s if we still have them, as I hope we shall. The 1966s should not need broaching until a full five years old. The best vintage of the decade was 1961, and these ought still be wines to guard; until the 1969s show their worth there is nothing so good to succeed them. For white burgundies we may rely on 1966s and 1967s, although fine French-bottled 1964s should still be excellent. Earlier years must be a toss-up.

Among clarets, the most suitable years might be 1962s and lesser 1964s for low days, and 1959s and 1961s, just reaching their first ten years, for high days. But the 1961s, accepted as the successors to the more problematical 1945s in the sequence of outstanding years, should not be rushed at; the quality was high but the quantity small, and the wines will soon be irreplaceable. No equally fine vintage has since emerged. There is probably no point in keeping further any other vintages of the fifties, with the possible exception of the still residually hard 1952s. However, although the 1955s may not improve much, perhaps with the exception of front-rank Pauillacs, there should be no need to hurry their departure, still less of the charming 1953s, provided they were well bottled. (Château-bottling is usually a reasonable guarantee.) So long as these wines keep their fruit, they and their seniors of the nineteen-forties are worth keeping for special occasions.

The sweet white Bordeaux have had such a disappointing decade in the nineteen-sixties that no great year emerged, for buying or drinking. The 1961s and 1962s were probably the best, followed by 1967.

On the other hand, the Germans had an unexpectedly successful period, in that although no vintage was as great as 1959, fine wines were made in 1964, 1966 and 1969, and acceptable ones in 1961, 1962 and 1967. Except for wines of *auslese* quality and above, 1966 is probably the oldest year to drink.

During the fifteen years that followed the last war, far too much young vintage port was consumed; so the years that should now be ready are rare indeed. The best of these is 1948, followed by 1945, particularly scarce as most was bottled in Oporto rather than here. The 1955s still seem so big that they should be left in peace for a few more years, and the lighter 1958s drunk; perhaps even some of the 1960s too, which show very forward.

It is to be hoped that these suggestions on buying and drinking do not appear too pontifical. Wine is so variable, so uncertain in its development, and subject to accidents of which we consumers probably know nothing, from the first day of fermentation onwards. We may be surprised that so many of these fine, almost 'hand-made' wines turn out so well; but then that is one of the reasons why some of us collect them.

For a Wine Festival

Now the late fruits are in.
Now moves the leaf-starred year
Down, in the sun's decline.
Stoop. Have no fear.
Glance at the burdened tree:
Dark is the grape's wild skin.
Dance, limbs, be free.
Bring the bright clusters here
And crush them into wine.

Acorns from yellow boughs
Drop to the listening ground.
Spirits who never tire,
Dance, dance your round.
Old roots, old thoughts and dry,
Catch, as your footprints rouse
Flames where they fly,
Knowing the year has found
Its own more secret fire.

Nothing supreme shall pass.
Earth to an ember gone
Wears but the death it feigns
And still burns on.
One note more true than time
And shattered falls his glass.
Steal, steal from rhyme:
Take from the glass that shone
The vintage that remains.